INNER BUSHIDO

STRENGTH WITHOUT CONFLICT

SEAN HANNON

Copyright 2014 by the author of this book Sean Hannon.
The book author retains sole copyright to
his contributions to this book.

All rights reserved. Published 2014.
Printed in the United States of America by Lightning Source Inc.

All rights reserved. No portion of this book may be reproduced, stored in a retrieval system, or transmitted in any form or by any means – electronic, mechanical, photocopy, recording, scanning, or other – except for brief quotations in critical reviews or articles, without the prior written permission of the author.

ISBN 978-0-9915646-0-6

Library of Congress Control Number 2014933164

This book was published by BookCrafters,
http://bookcrafters.net - bookcrafters@comcast.net

This book may be ordered from
www.bookcrafters.net and other online bookstores.

Portions of this book were previously distributed through
Castle Rock AIKIDO's blog:
http://craikido.blogspot.com and/or
website www.CRaikido.com.

Sketches by Peter Alexander
Author photograph by Daemon Donigan
Cover artist - Utagawa Kuniyoshi (1797 – 1861)

Hannon decisively strips away much of the dogma permeating martial arts today... Inner Bushido is a must read for all martial art practitioners interested in truly understanding and appreciating modern day Bushido!

– Tip Harris Sensei, Aikido Black Belt
Pikes Peak Aikido, Colorado, USA

Inner Bushido poses important comparisons about how Bushido's virtues came to be and how they are (and how they can be) interpreted in modern society. This book represents another evolution for the concept of yin and yang; hard and soft, old and new.

– Ryan Goettsche Sensei, Aikido Black Belt
Aikido Koshin Shuri, Colorado, USA

Hannon does what we should all do as we mature from the enthusiastic amateur to someone for whom martial arts have become a way of life. He lets go of the sacred cows, exotic terminology, and blind faith mythos to ask himself with brutal honesty what values it is he is pursuing, teaching, and propagating in this world. This book is a worthy read for any martial artist, but in particular should be required reading for those studying any art that ends with "-DO."

– Thomas Groendal Sensei, Jodo Black Belt
Hoshu Dojo, Oregon, USA

Hannon's work offers a thought-provoking perspective and examination of the Samurai code of ethics and morals and how they relate to the present day martial artist. It is a philosophical journey that helps one to both understand Bushido from a historical perspective and to apply the qualities that one values as a martial artist to everyday life. Anyone who practices martial arts, both inside and outside the dojo, would benefit from gaining a better understanding of Bushido through Hannon's analysis.

– Skip Chapman, Aikido Black Belt
Jersey Shore Aikikai, New Jersey, USA

(Hannon's book is) ...a thoughtful revisioning of such essential qualities as politeness or manners, honor, and loyalty. When practice is based on developing these and other virtues discussed in this book, it can transcend ordinary notions of competition, aggression, and pride. Then, martial arts practice becomes truly meaningful.

(The book is) a good antidote for the violence and foolishness that is often associated with training in the skills of warriorship and mastery of traditional "weapons." All serious practitioners will be grateful to see the publication of this fine, gentle and accessible book.

– Alex Halpern, Japanese Archery (Kyudo) Instructor
Zenko Kyudojo, Colorado, USA

Hannon breaks down the most core precepts of Bushido and puts them on trial... Anyone who actively discusses Bushido or considers it a real part of their life should consider this book a must.

– Matthew Apsokardu Sensei, Okinawa Kenpo Karate
Pennsylvania, USA

This is a great book! ... Clear and concise, interesting and dynamic.

– Victor Hung Sensei, Aikido Black Belt
Aikido of Colorado, Colorado, USA

Sean articulates the virtues of Bushido for the modern day warrior - bringing tradition together with the evolution of the true martial artist.

– Bruce Heckathorn Sensei, Aikido Black Belt
Aikido for Veterans, Colorado, USA

Winner 2014

Colorado Independent
Publishers Association

CIPA EVVY Award

Categories:

Social Science
Non-Fiction

TABLE OF CONTENTS

AUTHOR'S NOTE..iii
ACKNOWLEDGEMENTS......................................v
FOREWORD...vii
INTRODUCTION...1
CHAPTER 1:
The Origins of Bushido..5
CHAPTER 2:
Rectitude or 'Gi' - Living Free From Guilt........19
CHAPTER 3:
Courage or 'Yuu' - Doing the Hard Thing........29
CHAPTER 4:
Benevolence or 'Jin' - Feeling Distress for Others............37
CHAPTER 5:
Politeness or 'Rei' - Power in Repose................47
CHAPTER 6:
Truthfulness or 'Makoto' - One's Perfect Word..............57
CHAPTER 7:
Honor or 'Meiyo' - Self-Respect..........................71
CHAPTER 8:
Loyalty or 'Chuugi' - Listening to One's Highest Self...87
CHAPTER 9:
Transition & Evolution......................................105
BONUS CHAPTER:
Truthfulness (continued) - Bushido & Commerce........119
ABOUT THE AUTHOR.......................................128

AUTHOR'S NOTE

It was never my intent to publish this material in a printed book. These essays were simply an exercise of personal exploration and later served as a series of articles on our Aikido school's website. However, after receiving many e-mails from martial arts students and teachers from around the United States and other countries suggesting that I publish them in a book, I have finally, and somewhat reluctantly, conceded.

This book is a small effort intended to help bridge a large gap that exists between what Bushido was, is, and should be with what many in Western martial arts communities presently and erroneously think Bushido is. It is my opinion that Bushido is far too often an unfairly-utilized shield to hide behind rather than what I have always believed it to be; which is a valuable tool for growth and self-realization. I hope this book will allow for more people to enjoy these essays and possibly contribute to a better understanding of Bushido in the 21st century.

References to the martial arts throughout this book are often expressed within a context of Japanese Aikido since that is my primary martial arts experience. Japanese words that are less colloquial to Western readers are represented in 'single quotes' and are often accompanied by phonetic notation to assist in readability.

ACKNOWLEDGEMENTS

Thank you to the committed instructors and students at Castle Rock AIKIDO in Castle Rock, Colorado, USA. Specifically, I'd like to acknowledge my teachers: Tip Harris Sensei, Ryan Goettsche Sensei, Iwakabe, Monica Sensei, Iwakabe, Hideki Sensei, Mike Pattarozzi, and the many other people I've had the privilege of training martial arts with over the past twenty-plus years.

Thank you to my fellow martial arts students Kriss Myer, Peter Alexander, Tim Keating, and Len Silverston for their continued support and trust of our grand experiment. Your friendship, commitment, and wisdom over the years will never be forgotten.

Thank you also to my friend JD Paul Sensei of Steamboat Springs Martial Arts in Steamboat Springs, Colorado for setting a "Howard Roark-like" example, an inspiration for which I think he is completely unaware.

Thank you to Yoko Ondrejka for her assistance with the book's Japanese 'Kanji' and to Peter Alexander for his beautiful illustrations that appear throughout.

Thank you to Skip and Paige Chapman Sensei of

Jersey Shore Aikikai for their years of cross-continental friendship, business advisement, and promotion of our unorthodox 'Dojo.'

Thank you to Greg O'Connor Sensei of Aikido Centers of New Jersey for introducing me to the art of Aikido in the 1990s. Thank you to Rick and Mary Kay Scucci for their older sibling-like guidance, confidence, and friendship in the early-stages of my martial arts training. And thank you to my parents, Bruce and Jane Hannon, for their innate understanding and teaching of Bushido even though neither one of them has ever trained a day of martial arts in their lives.

FOREWORD

When Sean Hannon asked me to write the foreword for his book, *Inner Bushido*, I felt honored, and an interesting question arose. Given my recent ordination as a Zen priest in the Japanese 'Rinzai' tradition and specifically in the "Hollow Bones" order, the question arose about how much praise to give to Sean and his present work? In American culture, praise is seen as "good," but we have a saying in Zen that "praise is poison" because of how praise has a tendency to dissuade humility and create ego problems in some people. However, I have known Sean for several years and I can tell you that he is quick to acknowledge his own faults and errors (to which he will tell you there are many) and so I feel confident that the few words of praise contained in these paragraphs will probably not do too much harm.

Sean is a warrior. In the years that I have known him, I believe that he has embodied many aspects of the seven virtues of Bushido more fully than most people – those being Rectitude, Courage, Benevolence, Politeness, Truthfulness, Honor and Loyalty. So it is no wonder to me that he would be drawn to this code, and would write a book pondering and even challenging the applicability of these historical Samurai tenets in today's world. It seems to me that we all possess these qualities to one degree or another and also that there is room for improvement for all of us regarding these qualities.

A dictionary defines Rectitude as the "quality of being straight, moral integrity, righteousness or the quality or state of being correct in judgment." The way that Sean runs our Aikido and Iaido martial arts school in Castle Rock, Colorado, with fair, consistent policies and rules demonstrates, in my opinion, a very high level of integrity and straight-forwardness. Regarding Courage, it is amazing to me to witness a man like Sean (who had previously been crippled by a severe spine injury, unable to walk for over a year) still approach Aikido with such tremendous gusto, taking full-force break falls and all. The quality of Benevolence or "the disposition to do good" is evident is his actions, as well. For example, Sean has developed an Aikido program for teenagers where it is obvious that he does this primarily for the benefit of others, including my daughter, who learned a great deal from the classes. Sean demonstrates the quality of Politeness, which includes proper manners and etiquette, in the graceful and respectful way he moves, bows, addresses and treats others.

In Sean's other upcoming book on health, Sean fiercely addresses Truthfulness regarding health, fitness, and diet. In that book he cuts to the chase with piercing honesty that generates valuable insight to a reader. I have found my personal interactions with Sean to be the same and he is a man of great Veracity. Inazo Nitobe, author of *Bushido: The Soul of Japan*, describes Honor as *"a vivid consciousness of personal dignity,"* which is in stark contrast to other definitions of Honor that involve what other people think of you. Nitobe suggests that Honor is more closely aligned with what one thinks of oneself rather than how we are perceived by others. Sean carries himself with a personal pride and self-respect that demonstrates an inner, subtle confidence. Lastly, Sean proposes that instead of following traditional Japanese feudal customs of Loyalty to superiors, it may be more appropriate to exercise Loyalty in today's society as "an intra-personal dynamic" or "self-Loyalty," and to be loyal to "one's fundamental understanding of right and wrong," as well as "the command of a higher voice." In my experience, Sean lives his life this way, as well.

I am so grateful for this work that Sean offers to us, which he cultivated with a reverent spirit. The book *Inner Bushido* has provided me with additional insights to my own career and writings on corporate human dynamics. Prior to reading Sean's book, I had not fully considered Bushido as a potential resource for my work and my clients, but I can see its value and applicability much more clearly now. I hope you benefit from this book as I certainly did.

Kensho Len Silverston
Author, Speaker, and Zen Priest

For more information about Kensho Len Silverston visit:
www.ZenwithLen.com
www.universaldatamodels.com

INTRODUCTION

I've heard it said that most people never read past the first chapter of any book they start. If this is even remotely accurate, especially if one doesn't care for what they read, then I should state plainly and outright that I am a strong proponent and advocate of Bushido. My criticisms are not an attack on Bushido itself; rather, I am challenging what I believe to be an average Western person's understanding, use, and abuse of this potentially powerful system of values and thought.

Some might want to criticize me for having the audacity to evaluate Bushido having not lived in Japan. However, I hope it will become clear that the virtues of Bushido are not unique to Japan. The Samurai are extinct, yet people from all over the world claim to practice Bushido. So, Bushido can't possibly be unique to Japan. Nearly all cultures possess an equivalent values system essentially comprised of the same virtues. That is because these virtues are, in fact, virtues of humanity that transcend culture and ethnicity, so long as external forces such as a destructive religion or an oppressive government do not interfere with the expression of these innate virtues. Bushido's virtues are ubiquitous throughout the world and take many names including Chivalry, morals, ethics, the conduct of a gentleman, the Boy Scout's code of conduct and, of course, Bushido.

Some might challenge this literary effort by posing the question: *"Well, who gives you the right to edit, change, and evolve Bushido?"* The answer to that question is simple: the Japanese do. In Japanese culture there exists a concept strongly embraced by the overwhelming majority of the populace called 'Iitoko-dori' (pronounced 'ee'-'toh'-'koh'-'doh'-'rhee'). This is the Japanese tradition of adopting only the most useful and convenient elements of foreign concepts, technologies, and practices and rapidly adapting them to Japanese use — what Westerner's often call "cherry-picking." One of the best examples of 'Iitoko-dori' has been the successful integration and assimilation of the philosophies of Confucianism and Buddhism into the predominantly Shinto-based Japanese culture. Confucianism and Buddhism are both foreign systems of thought, from China and India, respectively. Yet, the Japanese embracement of 'Iitoko-dori' has enabled the country to peacefully coexist with these somewhat conflicting philosophies. The practice of 'Iitoko-dori' is also largely responsible for the rise of Japan's economic power throughout the last century. Like the Japanese, this book, too, embraces the notion of 'Iitoko-dori' by accepting those elements of feudal Bushido that still work in modern Western society, and adapting or even discarding those that simply do not.

Certainly some, perhaps many, with far more extensive education than me on this subject will disagree with some or all of my assessments. That's fine. However, the notions I present in this book are not wrong, they are just my opinions. You are welcome to your own.

CHAPTER ONE:
THE ORIGINS OF BUSHIDO

Many Western martial arts students and teachers have romantic notions of, and frequently espouse, the virtues of Bushido — the feudal, behavioral code of ancient Japanese Samurai. These individuals often claim to live and abide by such values and sometimes even pass judgment on themselves and others claiming Bushido as their standard of judgment. But do people today really know what those values were? Or, what those values might mean today? For example, some martial arts students and instructors profess unquestioned Loyalty as a virtue of Bushido. However, is unquestioned Loyalty always intelligent? If, at times, this is unintelligent then wouldn't that also suggest that Bushido, at times, is not intelligent?

And, what about Honor? Does Honor really exist as a

Inner Bushido

legitimate virtue? Or, is Honor just a more sophisticated way of inflating or defending one's ego? Are these and other alleged virtues of Samurai culture relevant outside of the oppressive, feudalistic society from which they emerged? Do people really understand these behavioral virtues as they existed? That is, do they understand them within a context of feudalism? Is it really possible to practice Bushido today as it was in the 11th through 19th centuries? Is it possible that Bushido is an antiquated system of values that is either no longer relevant today or, at the very least, is in need of adaptation and modernization? Can Bushido exist in cultural environments based on freedom, democracy, and capitalism? This book will explore questions like these and will propose possible answers for consideration. We will summarize Bushido's major principles, concepts, and values as articulated in the classic text, *Bushido: The Soul of Japan*, and evaluate their applicability in today's modern world.

Bushido: The Soul of Japan was written in 1899 by a Japanese national named Inazo Nitobe. His text is one of the first major works on Samurai ethics and Japanese culture. It is considered by some to be the first collective statement of what is commonly referred to as the seven virtues of Bushido. The book is considered significant, in part, because it was written during Japan's transition from its traditional lifestyle to a modern nation and, as stated in the book's dedication, its intent was to *"revere the past and to admire the deeds of the Samurai."* However, as we shall see, Nitobe's account of the Samurai is not unclouded by his Christian-academic background.

Nitobe converted to Christianity in early adulthood

The Origins of Bushido

while attending what is now Japan's Hokkaido University. At the time, the University was run by Christian missionaries and the book opens with a candid conversation between Nitobe and a fellow academic from Belgium. The Belgian asks Nitobe how Japanese children are educated on morality without monotheistic religion playing a part in their educational system. Nitobe replies that in Japan, Bushido, not religion, imparts moral precepts upon its children. Sensing confusion and astonishment from his colleague, Nitobe elaborates, strongly contending that one cannot possibly begin to understand the moral concepts of Japan without first understanding Bushido and the socio-economic system from which it arose: feudalism.

Unlike other classic Japanese texts surrounding Bushido or martial strategy that require translation from Japanese to English and are prone to contextual errors in translation, *Bushido: The Soul of Japan* was initially published in English, not Japanese. The book, originally published in Philadelphia, Pennsylvania, was specifically intended to educate non-Japanese about Japanese values. It has been read by many prominent Americans including U.S. Presidents Theodore Roosevelt and John F. Kennedy. It is also believed to have been highly influential in the development of the American Boy Scout movement.

Bushido was a system of values forged among the warrior class within the contextual environment of feudalism. Feudalism was a socio-economic and political system, which, in its most remedial of definitions, involved the granting of land by a monarch, governing lord, or other authority figure to members of lower classes

Inner Bushido

in return for military service. Feudalism represented a static social structure in which people were born, lived, and died within "their place" in society. Rising above that place where one was born in the social hierarchy was virtually unheard of. Each person was the servant of his or her lord. This concept can be challenging for Westerners since in our contemporary society, people are taught and encouraged from a very young age to make of themselves whatever they wish to be and to reach as high and as far as they can possibly imagine or desire. This is indeed the first hurdle one experiences when trying to live and practice Bushido today as it was practiced then.

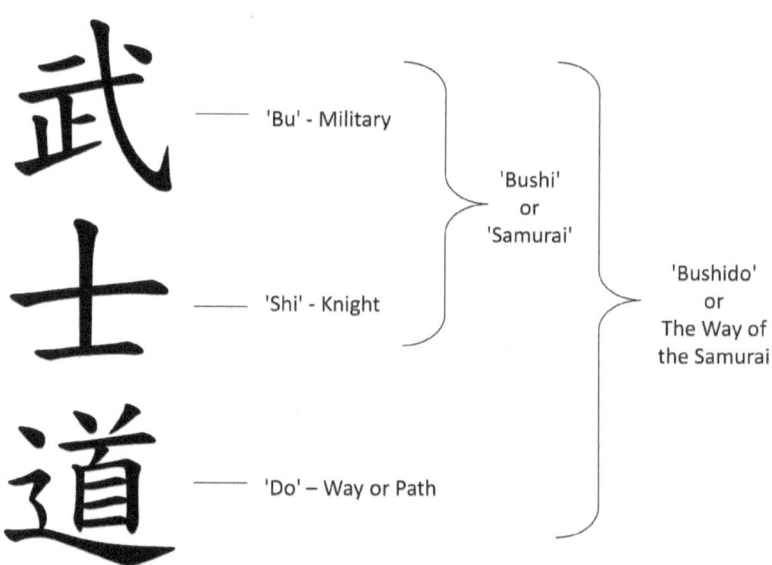

Nitobe makes the fairly accurate analogy that Chivalry is to Europe, as Bushido is to Japan. He appears to do this largely for the benefit of European and American

The Origins of Bushido

readers. 'Bu'-'shi'-'do' literally means "Military-Knight-Way." Or, said another way, the "Precepts of Knighthood." The "Way" was articulated, not necessarily in written word, but orally and behaviorally through customs. It was the conduct expected of Samurai in daily life — the code of moral principles Samurai were required to observe. Virtually an unwritten code consisting of nothing more than a few maxims handed down as an oral tradition from generation to generation, Bushido was a doctrine *"written on the fleshy tablets of the heart."* Nitobe further describes Bushido as an *"organic growth of decades and centuries of military career."* It would be nearly impossible to pinpoint Bushido's precise time, place, or person of origin. However, it can be accurately said that Bushido gradually developed out of an age of feudalism similar in time and manner to that of early European feudalism and Chivalry.

As "fighting knights" or 'Bushi,' Samurai were the natural leaders to arise as the prominent, military-nobility class in a feudalistic society. According to Nitobe, Samurai literally means "serving guards" or "attendants," and it was the Samurai who became the privileged class of the day. But with this great position of Honor and privilege gradually came the burden of responsibility, and from that, the need of a common standard of behavior so as to maintain social order and, hopefully, a pleasant way of life. The next logical question, then, is from where would this standard of behavior derive?

Bushido appears to be made up of two fundamental contributions: moral contributions and ethical contributions. The moral contributions of Bushido originate primarily from two sources: Buddhism and Shinto.

Inner Bushido

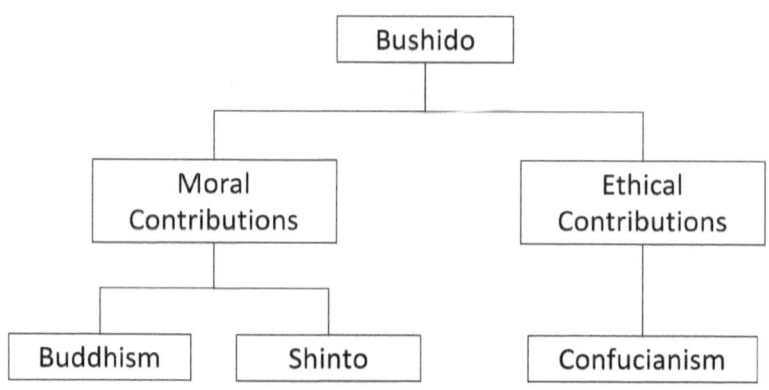

According to Nitobe, Buddhism *"furnished a sense of calm trust in Fate, a quiet submission to the inevitable, that stoic composure in sight of danger or calamity, that disdain for life and friendliness with death ... to put oneself in harmony with the Absolute."* Buddhism was a preferred source of how Samurai reconciled their mortality and was intended to satisfy their relationship with their Creator, with Life, or with the Universe. However, Buddhism by itself was insufficient.

What Buddhism lacked, Shinto offered in abundance — Loyalty to the sovereign and reverence for ancestral memory and filial piety. Having love and deep respect for one's parents and acting in accordance with the responsibilities that come with such respect is what Nitobe calls filial piety. Therefore, Shinto imparted *"passivity to the otherwise arrogant character of the Samurai,"* said Nitobe. Though categorized by some as a religion, Shinto contrasts starkly with religions of monotheistic origin like those that tend to dominate Western culture.

Having no room for any notion of "original sin," Shinto believes in the innate goodness and god-like purity of the human soul and adores the human soul as the vessel through which divine-like proclamations are made. Nitobe points out that (at least in the late 1800s) the primary article found in Shinto shrines is a plain mirror, rather than any object of worship representing a personified deity. The mirror is meant to symbolize the human heart, which when perfectly placid and clear reflects the very image of the deity — oneself, one's community, one's country, and one's world. The actual act of worship in Shinto, therefore, is equivalent to the popular axiom, *"Know thyself,"* not in the physiological sense, but in the context of introspection of one's moral nature.

According to Nitobe, the collective reflection of the Shinto-practicing Japanese is that of the *"national consciousness of the individual."* To the Japanese, the country is not just land and soil, but the *"sacred abode of the gods."* The land and the people are a collective deity in and of themselves. This profound, nature-worship distinction of Shinto is pervasive among the people. The Emperor of Japan is the highest authority of the Shinto religion. He is the symbol of the country and represents the unity of the people — the *"bodily representation of heaven on earth."* The Emperor of Japan is not a divine leader by proclamation of any deity, but is divine-like by unspoken agreement of the people.

When any pre-existing, religious connotation is removed from one's mind, it can be observed that Shinto, in fact, shares attributes similar to patriotism, or what Nitobe refers to as a *"national faith."* In fact, Americans might be able to best connect with the basic premise of Shinto by thinking of it more as patriotic, emotional feelings for one's country, rather than a theistic-based religion. Shinto is about reverence for this life and the lives of ancestral contributions. You might say that Shinto is about acknowledging the "here and now" and one's ancestral past as god-like. In contrast, monotheistic religions, like those predominating in the West, seem disproportionately preoccupied with preparing for death and the next life — the "elsewhere and later."

Monotheism	vs.	Shinto
concerned with the next life, the *"elsewhere and later"*		concerned with this life, the *"here and now"*

Bushido, then, is infused with two major tenets of Shinto: patriotism and Loyalty — Loyalty to the sovereign (i.e. the Emperor). Americans, for example, are frequently loyal to a sovereign-like figure such as a president, especially among military officers during times of war or the nation as a whole during times of great national achievement or crisis. However, America, having never really experienced a feudalistic-like society (although one could argue that black slavery may qualify as a form of feudalism) may struggle with the notion of Loyalty.

The predominant values in America are very different from that of feudalistic Japan. Since its inception, America's highest values have been freedom and individuality – not conformity like in Japan. In America, Loyalty to a "lord" or sovereign, be it the president of the country, the governor of a state, the mayor of a town, a martial arts instructor, or even a parent is limited, especially if such a sovereign behaves in a manner inconsistent with the expectations of their position. In stark contrast to the expectations of Japanese Samurai, it is not likely that you would ever find an American willing to die on the impulsive demand of a sovereign! How many of you would commit suicide at the request of Presidents George W. Bush or Barrack Obama? Not too many, I would think — even from the most avid of supporters. This is because American values are not congruent with those found in a feudalistic society. As such, one would be hard pressed to practice Bushido today as it was practiced in Japan's pre-industrial era. Even though today some may try to conduct their lives in a manner consistent with that of Japanese Bushido, Bushido certainly is not the dominating values system of today — and, nor should it be, one might convincingly argue. When threatened, most people today will default their actions and behavior to a more modern and independent system of values based on individual freedoms. This issue will be discussed and challenged further when each virtue of Bushido is critiqued individually.

The second fundamental contribution to Bushido is an ethical contribution. Its ethical contributions derive primarily from Confucianism and Confucius' disciples. Confucianism is the Chinese philosophical system focused on discerning between right and wrong action. This philosophy was particularly well suited to the Samurai class because Confucianism asserts that a community can be governed by moral virtue rather than be ruled by manipulative, punitive sets of laws. Mencius, a disciple of Confucius, expounded upon the concepts promulgated by his predecessor, but with a more adamantly democratic tone, particularly as they related to the innate goodness of human nature. Even though Mencius' teachings were under censure for a long time because of their inherent challenges to the existing social order and conformity, they still found *"permanent lodgment in the heart of the Samurai."*

Nitobe contends that a mere intellectual understanding of Confucian teachings was considered by Samurai to be inferior to *"ethical emotion."* According to his interpretation of Bushido, *"knowledge becomes really such only when it is assimilated in the mind of the learner and shows in his character."* Samurai would rationalize this dismissive attitude of a rote, academic mastery of Confucian analects with the famous axiom of another influential Chinese philosopher, Wan Yan Ming, *"To know and to act are one and the same."* Translation: Knowledge is only wisdom if acted upon. Or, to know and not to do is to not really know at all.

So, the sources of Bushido – Buddhism, Shinto, and Confucianism – were, as Nitobe suggested, simple and few. Yet these sources were sufficient enough *"to furnish a safe conduct of life even through the unsafest days of the most unsettled period of our [Japan's] history."* However, because Bushido existed in the context of a feudalistic society, I would argue that true Bushido, as it was originally practiced, cannot be experienced today as in earlier centuries despite alleged efforts by many, particularly those who study martial arts in the United States. Throughout this book, I will point out some of these cultural discrepancies and offer possible alterative interpretations and practices to what may indeed be an antiquated system of values in need of revision.

In the next seven chapters, we will review, in the

The Origins of Bushido

deliberate, linear order presented by Nitobe, the seven pervading characteristics or virtues of those who practiced Bushido during Japan's feudal period. Those seven virtues are:

1. Rectitude (or Justice) - 'Gi'
2. Courage - 'Yuu'
3. Benevolence - 'Jin'
4. Politeness - 'Rei'
5. Truthfulness (or Veracity) - 'Makoto'
6. Honor - 'Meiyo'
7. Loyalty - 'Chuugi'

Nitobe offers for consideration these seven virtues of Bushido that attempt to illustrate the philosophical values of the Samurai. He describes the seven virtues using the visual metaphor of a symmetrical arch with Loyalty as its keystone. We shall follow suit. I have created the illustration below to visually represent Nitobe's metaphor and have taken the liberty of including the three foundational, philosophical influences of Bushido: Confucianism, Buddhism, and Shinto.

However, it should be recognized that there are not, in actuality, seven virtues of Bushido. This is only Nitobe's subjective articulation of Samurai culture and it is little more than an artificial construct. Other academics like Nitobe or practitioners of Bushido could easily and perhaps in an equally comprehensive fashion offer four, ten, or even one-hundred virtues of Bushido.

Furthermore, the seven virtues presented here are concentric. That is, each value overlaps with and is influenced by another. No single virtue of Bushido

Inner Bushido

exists or can exist by itself. Remember, all systems of thought, including Bushido, are ultimately artificial. The holistic nature of any system of values is unlikely to be comprehensively articulated in written language. Some virtues transcend written word. Nonetheless, we will attempt to explore each thoroughly.

The Origins of Bushido

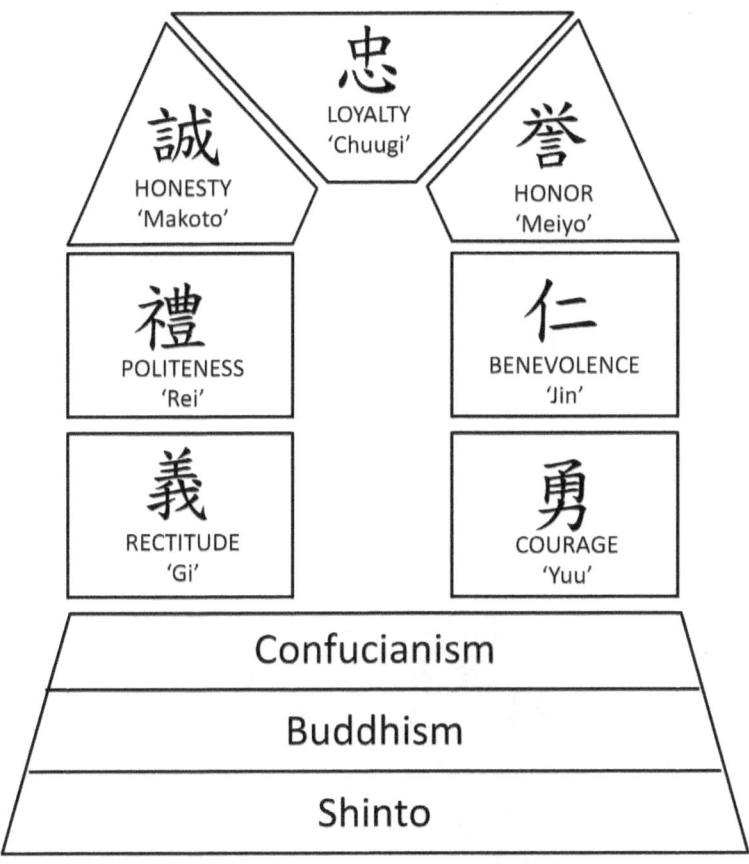

CHAPTER TWO: LIVING FREE FROM GUILT

RECTITUDE OR 'GI'

Nitobe begins his articulation of the seven virtues of Bushido with Rectitude or 'Gi' (pronounced 'ghee'). Rectitude is sometimes also referred to as Justice. He identifies Rectitude as the most cogent or powerfully-compelling precept in the code of the Samurai, and perhaps that is why he leads with this virtue. Nitobe immediately suggests that the word Rectitude may be too narrow a word to encompass the entirety of this virtue's meaning. He then expands his definition of 'Gi' to include the notion of righteousness. According to Mencius, the influential, post-Confucian Chinese philosopher introduced in the previous chapter, *"righteousness is a straight and narrow path which a man ought to take to regain the lost paradise."*

Inner Bushido

Nitobe quotes a famous 'Bushi' or Samurai warrior by saying that Rectitude is *"the power of deciding upon a certain course of conduct in accordance with reason, without wavering; to die when it is right to die, to strike when it is right to strike."* This suggests that a person possessing Rectitude is one who must be able and willing to effectuate sometimes difficult or unpleasant actions when and only when it is appropriate to do so. When a decision is made (within a context of right reasoning), and it is time to act, one must not waiver or hesitate. One must not act with a divided mind. He or she must act decisively; engage without compromise, and with full comprehension of the consequences and potential consequences of such action.

When I think of the *"straight and narrow path"* of Rectitude, I envision the attributes of a sword's blade. The blade's qualities of being straight and narrow produce its useful function of being sharp. Sharpness, however, does not necessarily connote anger, violence or otherwise ill intentions. Rather, it is meant to convey effectiveness. Rectitude is another way of implying direct effectiveness of one's actions. An anonymous contemporary of Nitobe describes Rectitude as *"the bone that gives firmness and stature ... [W]ithout Rectitude, neither talent nor learning can make of a human frame a Samurai."*

Nitobe says that *"Nothing is more loathsome to him [the Samurai] than underhand dealings and crooked undertakings."* This implies that the expression of Rectitude also entails virtuous, moral, and/or ethical conduct. Merriam-Webster's dictionary defines Rectitude as *"the quality of being straight, moral integrity, righteousness, or the quality or state of being correct in judgment or procedure."* However, these definitions are not definitive in that they then

Rectitude

beg the questions, "What is moral integrity?" "What is righteousness?" And, "How does one know if one is correct in judgment?" If we're being completely honest, these seemingly black and white questions do not necessarily come with black and white answers.

For example, according to Nitobe, a man of Rectitude is sometimes referred to by Japanese as 'Gishi' and this term was considered superior to any other term signifying mastery of an art or learned skill. The story of the 47 Faithful, considered by some to be the "national legend" of Japan, is a powerful tale based on actual events that Nitobe contends classically exemplifies the virtue of Rectitude in which 47 'Ronin' or lordless Samurai masterfully feigned their vengeful intent for over two years before justly avenging their lord or 'Daimyo.' After successfully infiltrating the well-protected residence and executing the person responsible for their master's death, these 47 'Ronin' were all subsequently ordered to commit ritual suicide or 'Seppuku' by the magistrate.

The 47 Faithful are commemorated for their ideal-most illustration of Rectitude because although their vengeful actions were technically illegal, necessitating the punishment of death, their actions were overwhelmingly considered just. That is, society as a whole recognizes that "right and wrong" and "legal and illegal" are not always and not necessarily congruent with one another. What the 47 Faithful did was illegal and, many would argue, was also the right and just thing to do. It is for this reason that these loyal Samurai demonstrating Rectitude are so revered in Japanese culture and, even to this day, are called the 47 'Gishi.' This timeless, compelling issue of *what to do when doing the right thing means doing something illegal* is a common and central theme in storytelling around the world, and serves as the basis for a seemingly unlimited number of films, books and cultural fables.

Now couldn't one argue that the actions of the 47 Faithful were inappropriate? Certainly. It just depends on how you look at it. I concur that what the 47 did was right and just. However, let's look at the situation from another perspective. Consider the likely fact that most of those 47 Faithful had spouses and children. These 'Ronin' were very aware of the fact that, if successful at their revenge, they would in all likelihood be subsequently required to commit suicide. That is, they were acutely aware of the consequences of their actions. Is leaving their spouses husbandless and their children fatherless a responsible action? Is this acting in accordance with right reasoning? Some might convincingly argue, no. Therefore, what constitutes Rectitude depends heavily on one's focus, perspective, and objective. One could easily argue that leaving so many spouses without resource and so many children fatherless is utterly irresponsible and does not meet Nitobe's definition of Rectitude. Certainly, these 47 Samurai *"decided upon a certain course of conduct,"* and executed that decision *"without wavering."* However did they do such *"in accordance with reason"* as Nitobe unambiguously states is a defining characteristic of Rectitude? In the absence of this crucial element, is Rectitude virtuous? Or is one just petulantly responding from one's ego?

Merriam-Webster continues to define righteousness as *"being free from guilt or sin"* and *"being justifiable."* I connect with the *"free from guilt"* definition of righteousness because it, in my opinion, really gets to the heart of the matter. In order to infuse oneself with the virtue of Rectitude, one must be able to be free from guilt of one's past actions. Or, perhaps in more practical terms, to be able to sleep soundly at night and not be kept up by regret of one's past decisions. Furthermore, righteousness might connote the ability to find value and wisdom in one's past actions, particularly in one's mistakes, and the willingness to make any necessary amends accordingly and in proportion to one's error. This emotionally-challenging process, I believe, is the narrow path to which Nitobe eludes.

But the larger question we are posing in this discussion of Bushido is: Is Bushido antiquated? As such, we must first ask: Is Rectitude antiquated? I believe the answer is, unequivocally, no. Rectitude is as important and relevant today as it has always been. However, its context may have changed. What was once considered righteous, just, and the possession of Rectitude in a feudal society may today be considered inappropriate or even irresponsible. For example, let's say that you are a Samurai of feudal Japan and your lord requests of you to do something that you deem inappropriate, unethical, or harmful to another. If violating the order of your lord is punishable by death of you and your family, is following that order righteous? Would your carrying out of that order be one of moral integrity? That would depend upon your values. Would carrying out the unethical order to save yourself and your family be conducting yourself in a manner consistent with Bushido? Or would refusing to carry out the unethical order and risking your own life and those of your family be considered conducting yourself in a manner consistent with Bushido?

Inner Bushido

Samurai were expected to demonstrate Loyalty (another virtue we'll explore at length in a later chapter), but they were also expected to possess Rectitude. What should a Samurai or a practitioner of Bushido do when doing the right thing means being disloyal? Can you see the conflict? In order then to demonstrate congruency in one's current understanding of feudal Bushido, an advocate might argue that the only proper thing to do in such a situation would be to commit suicide. However, I would argue that this certainly isn't demonstrating right reasoning and certainly not in a post-feudal world. To me, such an action would be just foolish. After all, isn't suicide the most cowardly way out of almost any situation?

Today, feudal socio-economic structures are virtually non-existent, particularly in Western societies. Therefore, in one's attempt to practice Bushido and exhibit Rectitude, one must ask what the standard of moral integrity is. To some this standard is, allegedly, stated plainly in sacred texts of monotheistic religions. To non-religious people or to people who practice non-deity-based religions or philosophies, this standard is often found viscerally, within oneself — what some people access by calling upon one's "highest self" or "deepest self." Japanese Shinto, embraced by Bushido, believes that moral integrity is the product of the innate goodness of a person when his or her mind is calm and still. This would be one such means of determining righteous action or thought.

Before departing from Rectitude, Nitobe addresses an element of Rectitude he believes has been perverted in popular acceptance among Japanese culture (at least in the late 1800s). Personally, I believe that this perversion of Rectitude still dominates in Western martial arts communities of today. That perversion can be found in the notion of 'Giri' (pronounced 'ghee'-'ree').

'Giri' is often loosely defined as the "duty" or "obligation" one has to a person or to an institution of one kind or another. As such, many people, particularly those who practice martial arts in the United States, often take great license with the use of this term and its consequence. According to Nitobe, the original definition of 'Giri' was simply *"what right reason demands and commands us to do."* An example of demonstrating 'Giri' would include the caring for your elderly parents in return for their taking care of you while growing up. This duty or obligation, Nitobe would contend, is what right reason demands us to do if the motive of love is inadequate or absent.

However, Nitobe suggests that 'Giri' has been twisted and distorted into something perverse — *"a vague sense of duty which public opinion expected one to fulfill."* Or, stated in other words, 'Giri' became what *public consensus* demands and commands us to do, as opposed to what *right reason* demands and commands us to do. 'Giri' became a person's conforming to consensus out of fear of public censure. The imperative of right and wrong was somehow eliminated from the understanding of 'Giri.' For example, what if a parent was physically or sexually abusive to their child? Does that child still have an obligation or duty to care for that parent in their elder years? If the public were not aware of such personal violations and immoral behavior, might not some prematurely and erroneously pass uninformed judgment

Inner Bushido

on the grown child for not exhibiting appropriate 'Giri' toward their parent? This is just a reminder to us all to try to reserve judgment of others when we do not have complete facts at our disposal.

In fact, in the above example, I would agree with Nitobe's objection to the perversion of 'Giri' and argue that this grown child may, in fact, be demonstrating correct 'Giri' toward the abusive parent in that the parent's dishonorable actions void and forfeit any duty or obligation the grown child might have to care for the parent. Right reason demands such, and, therefore, proper 'Giri' is being fulfilled. According to Nitobe, *"Carried beyond or below right reason, 'Giri' ... harbored under its wings every sort of sophistry [deception] and hypocrisy."*

The notion of Rectitude suggests that when we find ourselves out of alignment with our own personal values, we must raise our consciousness enough to first recognize the discord, and second, find within us the personal strength to follow a strict and narrow course of action congruent with the values we wish to live by and exhibit. In a word ... discipline. Discipline is the one and only path to Rectitude — and it is, indeed, a narrow path that few people choose to follow. Much easier is it to select a wider, more-traveled road.

As you can see, the demonstration of Rectitude can be most challenging. This may be why Nitobe describes Rectitude as a *"narrow"* path, and we all know how narrow, steep paths can be quite scary at times. Therefore, as you can probably anticipate, Rectitude has a prerequisite: Courage. In the next chapter, we will explore the second of the seven virtues of Bushido, 'Yuu' or Courage — what Nitobe calls Rectitude's *"twin brother."*

Rectitude

So, what can we take away from this discussion? How can we practice Bushido and demonstrate Rectitude or 'Gi' in our lives right now and today? We can recognize that:

1. **Rectitude is something you give to yourself; not something that is bestowed upon you by others;**
2. **Rectitude means living your life by a standard of personal moral integrity rooted in 'Giri' or right reasoning, not public consensus; and**
3. **Rectitude is a challenging narrow path of deliberate, disciplined actions that causes you to live without guilt.**

CHAPTER THREE: DOING THE HARD THING

COURAGE OR 'YUU'

Nitobe begins his discussion of Courage or 'Yuu' (pronounced 'yoo') by identifying it as the element responsible for preserving 'Giri,' a concept discussed in the previous chapter, and an attribute parallel to Rectitude. He says, *"Giri might easily have been turned into a nest of cowardice, if Bushido had not a keen and correct sense of Courage."*

Before defining the Courage associated with Bushido, Nitobe first summarizes a popular conception of *Physical* Courage, describing it as *"the spirit of daring and bearing,"* but notes that this is a quality of the soul *"which appeals most easily to juvenile minds."* He continues to say that *"rushing into the jaws of death"* is a frequently cited example of Courage, but that *"such rashness of conduct is unjustly applauded."*

Clearly, Nitobe would not find value in the so-called "Courage" that Hollywood frequently attempts to illustrate in martial arts and other war-related movies of today. Nitobe then goes on to further distinguish *Physical* Courage from *Moral* Courage and he implies that Moral Courage is far superior. For example, he quotes another figure from Japanese history, *"To rush into the thick of battle and to be slain in it is easy enough, and the merest churl is equal to the task."* The contemporary then continues with a contrasting remark, *"…but it is true courage to live when it is right to live, and to die only when it is right to die."* This quote is frequently butchered in Hollywood and in other examples of contemporary society leaving only the later portion relating to death. Rarely, if ever, is Courage accurately expressed as *"living when it is right to live."* Hollywood is clearly much more interested in emphasizing the death notion of this virtue, perhaps for dramatic and cinematic purposes.

Many Bushido enthusiasts may be surprised to discover that unless Courage was exercised in the cause of righteousness, Courage was scarcely deemed virtuous in the values system of Bushido according to Nitobe. Again, righteousness or Rectitude is the taking of action in accordance with right reasoning and without guilt. Nitobe is assisted by both Plato and Confucius in defining Courage, but in short, summarizes Courage as *"doing what is right."* This, Nitobe would identify as Moral Courage. A modern day author, Larry Winget, articulates a similar sentiment. He says that whenever you are faced with a choice between two actions, the right decision is always, and without fail, the harder of the two actions. Deciding to do the harder of those actions means to act with Courage and in a righteous fashion. Very few people today consistently choose to do the hard thing. Therefore, few people exhibit the moral expression of Courage. Courage occurs in the immaterial world — the mind and spirit — while Rectitude takes place in the material world — the actions that carry out one's courageous thoughts. Or, put another way, Courage means doing what is right in the moment and Rectitude is physically practicing the discipline and perseverance associated with emphatically carrying out what is right over time.

Plato defines Courage as *"the knowledge of things that a man should fear and that he should not fear."* This implies that knowledge is an ingredient of Courage. Furthermore, *"The spiritual aspect of valor is evidenced by composure — calm presence of mind. Tranquility is Courage in repose."* Nitobe continues, *"A truly brave man is ever serene; he is never taken by surprise; nothing ruffles the equanimity of his spirit. In the heart of battle he remains cool."* This passage implies that composure is a second ingredient of Courage.

So, one must logically now ask, how does one possess a calm presence of mind and tranquility? I would offer for consideration that both preparation and repetition precede composure, for when we know what to expect, and have done something with abundant repetition it is far easier to remain calm. Have you ever seen someone on an airplane for the first time nervous and upset? Why? It's because they probably aren't prepared for the experience. But look at those frequent flier businesspersons who practically live in the sky. They can sleep and relax through even the most turbulent of

Inner Bushido

flights. Courage then, I would contend, is a product of knowledge and composure; and that composure is the product of preparation and repetition. When combined, knowledge, preparation, and repetition create order and certainty. Order and certainty help one demonstrate the composure associated with Courage. This also means that Courage is formulaic and can be acquired. We are not necessarily born courageous.

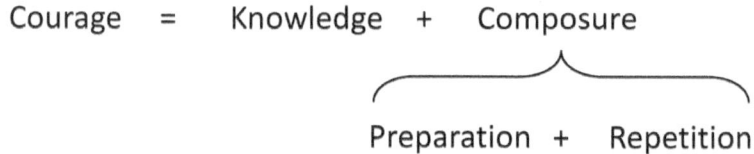

Courage = Knowledge + Composure

Preparation + Repetition

This is a formula historically used in all martial arts training with particular emphasis on the element of repetition. Over and over, martial arts students practice their 'Kata,' their techniques, their breathing and energy extension exercises, and their sparring. It is through this endless, disciplined repetition that non-intuitive responses become viscerally-automated with exacting precision in the musculature and nervous systems of practitioners. On the Aikido mat, for example, is one who can repeatedly, calmly, expertly, and seemingly effortlessly take full force break falls without sustaining injury or becoming exhausted exhibiting Courage? Or, does that student merely have knowledge and composure produced through repetition?

If ever one is unfortunate enough to unexpectedly find themselves in a life-threatening situation requiring a decisive, violent response, that knowledge, preparation, and repetition instantaneously integrate and commence with Rectitude to resolve the crisis. Only after the fact, whether successful or unsuccessful, do others witnessing or otherwise not involved in addressing the threat describe the response of those who did act as courageous.

Courage then, one could also argue, may be a relative concept because one only *appears* courageous in front of others who lack order and certainty due to their of lack of knowledge and composure. For example, eccentric American scientist, Nikola Tesla, at the turn of the 20th century must have certainly appeared courageous to the masses as he, it was reported, would "fearlessly" walk through giant arcs and bolts of man-made electricity in public demonstrations in New York, Chicago, and Colorado Springs. No doubt, these feats appeared to be "death-defying" in the early 20th century. Tesla certainly must have been perceived as a courageous individual. However, wasn't Tesla's Courage really a product of his mastery of the force of lightning? This then raises the question: If one behaves calmly and with serenity of mind, and no one is around to witness it, is that man indeed courageous? Does the existence of Courage require at least two parties: one exhibiting Courage (knowledge and composure) and the other lacking one or both of these qualities?

Either way, the Moral Courage, as presented by Nitobe, is radically different than the Physical Courage commonly presented in Hollywood movies about Samurai, combat or war. So, is Courage an antiquated virtue? That would depend on your definition of Courage. If you define Courage as Physical Courage, similar to its representation in Hollywood, then I would answer in the affirmative. In many cases, Courage is an antiquated value. However, if you define Courage as Moral Courage, as Nitobe does, then I would strongly answer in the negative. Courage is not an antiquated virtue of Bushido.

What can we take away from this discussion? How can we practice Bushido and demonstrate Courage or 'Yuu' in our lives right now and today? We can recognize that:

1. **Courage isn't necessarily blindly attacking the enemy. True Courage is to live when it is right to live; and is only virtuous when exercised in a righteous endeavor;**
2. **Moral Courage means doing what is right, which also means doing the hard thing; and**
3. **Courage is a product of knowledge, preparation, and repetition; these latter two elements make up Courage's inherent quality of composure, which allows one to demonstrate a calm presence of mind during times of stress and disorder.**

When Courage is exhibited in its highest capacity, it becomes akin to Benevolence. We shall address that virtue in the next chapter.

Courage

CHAPTER FOUR: FEELING DISTRESS FOR OTHERS

BENEVOLENCE OR 'JIN'

"The bravest are the tenderest; the loving are the daring."
— Inazo Nitobe

This next virtue of Bushido is what I consider "the forgotten virtue" because it is possibly one of the least likely virtues one might expect of a warrior. However, Chinese philosophers, Confucius and Mencius, thought Benevolence or 'Jin' (pronounced 'jee-n') to be the highest requirement of a ruler of men and Nitobe describes it as *"the highest of all the attributes of the human soul."* Strange then that it should be a virtue so easily dismissed by most. When people such as those in martial arts purport

Inner Bushido

to follow or teach Bushido, this virtue of Benevolence, I believe, is often overlooked or merely given lip service. Rarely is such a virtue considered a powerful factor in guiding moral behavior among average, every day people of today, or even a ruling class like the Samurai of yesteryear.

I imagine that Benevolence might have been one of Morihei Ueshiba's (The Founder of Aikido) favorite or most-valued virtues of Bushido. The way we Aikido practitioners consistently practice restraint in the amount of force used, in my opinion, is one demonstration of Benevolence. For when we practice Aikido, although a powerful martial art, we do not practice in a manner that leads to serious injury of our partner. Of course, we are prepared, willing and able to exercise less restraint should a real self-defense situation require such, but, by and large, we elect to utilize as little aggression as possible.

Benevolence is a word that isn't necessarily used by many in daily conversation. So perhaps we should define it. Merriam-Webster's dictionary defines Benevolence as *"the disposition to do good,"* or *"an act of kindness."* It is also defined as *"charity motivated by sympathy, understanding and generosity."* Nitobe succinctly defines Benevolence as *"feeling distress for others."* However, when one conjures up their classical, bellicose image of a Samurai, Benevolence may not be the first attribute to come to mind.

A Samurai's demonstration of Benevolence implied the exhibition of mercy, especially when the granting of mercy in a particular situation was not the instinctive impulse. Or, in other words, despite being granted the authority to kill right on the spot for an offense, it was a true Samurai demonstrating Bushido who elected to

Benevolence

forgive, ignore, let go, or otherwise grant mercy to that offense.

I remember watching the 1980s television mini-series, *Shogun*, starring Richard Chamberlain, based on the book of the same title by author James Clavell, where a very different portrayal of so-called Bushido was presented. In one of the opening scenes, a peasant was suddenly beheaded by an angry, passing Samurai for not paying the proper respect to him. This, of course, was a perverted example of Bushido and, in fact, was not Bushido at all. According to Nitobe, a much more Benevolent response by the Samurai, in accordance with the virtues of Bushido, might have been to forgive the peasant, simply ignore him, or perhaps be satisfied by giving a stern, disapproving look. This fictitious warrior clearly lacked Benevolence and, therefore, lacked Bushido despite his designation as part of the Samurai class. Nitobe argues that having the power and authority to kill, but instead demonstrating restraint, is much more in accordance with Bushido – and instilling a strong sense of Benevolence was one way to cultivate this behavior.

This example, although fictitious, points out the likely fact that not all Samurai exhibited the virtues of Bushido, just as not all people, at all times, demonstrate their highest selves, sympathy for others, or best manners. Therefore, just because one may have been Samurai does not necessarily mean they were a good person or that they were virtuous. Bushido was an ideal, and therefore, like most ideals, may have been the exception instead of the rule. I think far too many Westerners erroneously assume that all or most Samurai lived up to this ideal of Bushido. This is certainly a most unrealistic expectation.

Inner Bushido

In short, Benevolence is the conscious choice to exercise restraint both in verbal condemnation and in the carrying out of physical punishment. Just because Samurai had the right to kill commoners on the spot for any offense does not mean that it was appropriate to exercise such a right. To do such was not a demonstration of Bushido, but rather a lack of it.

While Nitobe defines Benevolence as *"feeling distress for others,"* it would be valuable to acknowledge the importance of demonstrating Benevolence toward oneself, as well. Being able to forgive oneself for an oversight, misjudgment, or failure is an important behavior to cultivate. There are countless stories, true or not, about Samurai who, by Western standards, overreact to seemingly trivial, benign failures of one kind or another and are all too quick to offer to forfeit their lives or even just cut off a finger in redress. Such an excessive response to failure is perplexing to say the least to most of Western society. I, for one, was never impressed by this kind of an excessive, flippant offering and can't imagine why such a disposition would be considered congruent with Bushido.

When seeing examples of this in film or on television, I have always failed to perceive it as a polite gesture, but instead was more often than not embarrassed by its ridiculous disproportion. I fail to see how this kind of behavior demonstrates the *"right reasoning"* attribute of Rectitude or the *"die only when it is right to die"* tenet of Courage. To me, right reasoning would be to at least keep the apology and reparation proportional to the alleged offense; and have the Courage to take up the responsibility of correcting the failure or offense, instead shunning the responsibility for cleaning up one's mistakes by offering to kill oneself, thus taking oneself out of consideration for resolution. Such circumstances where 'Seppuku' was the verdict were, in my opinion, overwhelmingly non-Benevolent and unbecoming of a follower of Bushido.

"Under the regime of feudalism, which could easily be perverted into militarism, it was to Benevolence that we [Japanese] owed our deliverance from tyranny of the worst kind," Nitobe contends. Although I am not convinced, Nitobe is confident that feudalism did function in a non-tyrannical fashion so long as rulers exhibited Benevolence. He continues to say that *"Virtue and absolute power may strike the Anglo-Saxon mind as terms which it is impossible to harmonize."* Nitobe accurately anticipates my objection as I, one of Anglo-Saxon descendent, definitely cannot conceive of these two elements coexisting.

In the West, we have a saying that *"Absolute power corrupts absolutely."* Apparently, as Nitobe hints, this was an issue among the Samurai, as well. The virtue of Benevolence appears to have been deliberately and somewhat posthumously infused into the lore of Bushido by Nitobe and possibly others before him, as the extended period of peace prior to the Meiji Restoration of the late 19th century called for a reevaluation of the purpose and usefulness of the Samurai class. Thus, the Benevolence virtue was an effort to bring civility, sophistication, and gentleness to a class of warriors who prided themselves on their brute force, but increasingly found such assets inadequate in the face of increasing societal and non-war related responsibilities. Benevolence, therefore, was introduced to Bushido to prevent a Samurai from abusing his power and position in society and to, in fact, remember his own place and exercise restraint accordingly. Benevolence supplies modesty and perspective to the importance of one's position as it relates to the rest of society. It keeps a Samurai "in check," so to speak.

Nonetheless, it is evident that Benevolence is a virtue that easily transcends its socio-political and socio-economic environment, functioning well in feudalism, socialism, or democracy. Indeed, its tender, mother-like characteristics act as an alkalizing buffer for any acidic social environment. As such, Benevolence is definitely the least sexy, the least alluring, and perhaps, the least valued in a context of warrior-ship. However, after studying *Bushido: The Soul of Japan*, it seems that an appreciation for Benevolence may be the defining quality that differentiates a person who lives Bushido from a person who does not.

In his previous discussion on Courage, Nitobe details a profoundly respectful relationship between two feuding Samurai and states, *"when valor attains this [supreme] height, it becomes akin to benevolence."* This assertion, to me, was more interesting than the virtue itself. After all, I don't know how one could object to or challenge, in and of itself, the value of Benevolence. However, the notion that Benevolence is *"Courage at its highest"* is thought-provoking and implies that Courage is, in fact, a prerequisite to Benevolence. That is, one must have the Courage to feel distress for others before one can act benevolently. This was something I had not previous considered.

Benevolence brought balance to the character of a Samurai. If Rectitude was to be considered stern, upright, and masculine, then Benevolence was deliberately

Benevolence

injected into Bushido to cultivate the gentle, pliant, and feminine qualities thought to be ideal in the Samurai class. Benevolence softened the sharp edges and corners of Rectitude. It is interesting to note that these gentler qualities of Bushido are heavily de-emphasized or even completely absent in many Western martial arts schools today. This virtue, perhaps, keeps one from being perceived as overly neurotic or excessive in their observance of other virtues like Rectitude and lower expressions of Courage. Another way of expressing this concept could be: Benevolence is to 'Yin' as Rectitude is to 'Yang.' Together they create a healthy and dynamic equilibrium. Nitobe said, *"Rectitude carried to excess hardens into stiffness; Benevolence indulged beyond measure sinks into weakness."* Perhaps, this is a dynamic we should all keep in mind.

We can all benefit from this virtue by recognizing that one does not have to practice martial arts to demonstrate Bushido. Certainly anyone, functioning in any capacity or role, whether a parent, spouse, employee, teacher, or whatever, innately possesses the power, skills, and awareness to demonstrate Benevolence or any other virtue associated with Bushido. We merely must decide to do so.

Nitobe quotes Frederick the Great that *"Kings are the first servants of the state."* I recognize this to analogously mean, in a martial arts context, that the teachers or 'Sensei' are first servants to the students – and not the other way around – as is the unfortunate case in far too many martial arts schools or 'Dojo' in America and abroad. Some martial arts instructors confuse their role and responsibility, thinking that students are there to serve them! Nitobe clarifies the inverse. Of course, this is a mutually-reciprocating relationship that neither teacher nor student should take for granted.

How can we demonstrate Benevolence in our own Western lives today? Perhaps it is in how we treat our children when they misbehave, or how we respond to an upset co-worker, spouse or even an aging parent when they may occasionally lash out at us. I think, in short, one of the best ways to describe Benevolence can be concisely stated in a common aphorism: *"Try to see it from the other person's perspective."* Or, perhaps, *"Try walking in their shoes for a while."* Step outside of yourself and think about how you might feel if you were experiencing someone else's plight, and you just may find within yourself that *"feeling of distress for others"* that Nitobe defines as Benevolence – a required attribute of Bushido. Feeling distress for others or granting mercy for others doesn't necessarily mean that you indulge someone's inappropriate or unacceptable behavior, but perhaps only choose to modify your own response and not pass judgment too harshly on them.

As another example, poetry was deliberately introduced into a Samurai's education for the distinct purpose of cultivating a gentler warrior class. It was thought that *"the cultivation of tender feelings [would breed] considerate regard for the suffering of others."* Perhaps we can demonstrate this on the martial arts floor by choosing to be more patient when working with a newer student who is struggling with a basic technique.

So, is Benevolence an antiquated virtue of Bushido? Absolutely not. In fact, it may be more necessary today than ever, but is also, rather ironically, the most forgotten or ignored. Perhaps it is this way because Benevolence is not culturally unique to Bushido or to Japan, but is, or at least should be, a constant standard in all cultures. Perhaps the need for Benevolence in society is so ubiquitous that most of us fail to acknowledge its value and recognize its absence.

Much as Courage is a prerequisite to both Rectitude and Benevolence, Benevolence finds itself at the foundation for exploring the next virtue of Bushido: Politeness.

In summary, Benevolence or 'Jin' means:

1. **Having genuine feelings of distress and sympathy for the suffering of others;**
2. **Exercising restraint both in oral condemnation and in physical punishment of others; and**
3. **Being willing to forgive oneself for transgressions without disproportionate self-castigation.**

CHAPTER FIVE: POWER IN REPOSE

POLITENESS OR 'REI'

In and of itself, Politeness sounds like a boring virtue. It reminds me of my mother repeatedly telling me as a child to take my elbows off the dinner table. In fact, one might be tempted to skip this chapter for on the surface, it does not ring true to one's romantic illusions about Japanese Samurai and Bushido. However, such would surely be a mistake in judgment. Nitobe, as is becoming the norm, quickly intrigued me with a unique understanding of and application for this virtue. He warns that Politeness, Respect or 'Rei' (pronounced 'ray'-'ee') is a poor virtue if it is exercised merely out of fear of offending good taste or caring too much about what others think. Instead, Politeness should be *"the outward manifestation of a sympathetic regard for the feelings of others."* He continues,

Inner Bushido

"In its highest form, Politeness almost approaches love." Still, Nitobe does not gauge Politeness as superior to any other virtue of Bushido. Instead, he acknowledges its equivalency and complementarity to the others.

Certainly for many, Politeness may initially be perceived a peculiar virtue of warrior-ship. However, as has been discussed in a previous chapter, with the increasing status of the Samurai class came proportionally increasing degrees of societal responsibility. Politeness among this warrior class (and, in turn, the other classes, as well) was asserted to have been elevated to the pinnacle of social intercourse. Elaborate systems of etiquette and propriety (manners, if you will) came into vogue surrounding many common daily activities. For example, there became a best way to bow, to walk, to sit, to demonstrate table manners, and even a proper, ideal way to prepare and serve tea. *"A man of education is expected to be a master of all of these,"* Nitobe declares.

This attitude — this consciousness — surrounding the virtue of Politeness is not limited to how one behaves or conducts oneself in the presence of others. Self-Politeness is as much a reflection of how one respects oneself as it does others. Good hygiene, proper dress and appearance, and being physically fit are all signs of how much — or whether or not — one respects oneself. That quality of self-respect, in turn, spills over in the form of manners and in how or whether one respects others.

Nitobe is not alone in his opinion of Politeness. Famous Samurai, Yamamoto Tsunetomo from the 17th century book, *Hagakure* (a.k.a. Hidden Leaves), or more commonly known as *The Book of the Samurai*, emphasizes the importance of Politeness, manners, and self-respect

Politeness

when he is quoted as saying, *"Samurai ... without fail, pay attention to their personal appearance,"* and *"[i]t is because a Samurai has correct manners that he is admired."*

It must be recognized, however, that there are indeed, cultural differences regarding what is considered polite. For example, Nitobe states that in America and the West, we praise and appreciate gifts that are given. However, in Japan gifts are slandered and depreciated. In America, the logic is, *"Here is a nice gift. We would not dare give you a gift were it not nice,"* and that is why it is praised. In Japan, the logic is, *"No gift I give you could possibly be good enough for you,"* and that is why it is slandered. Ironically, although these two statements seem diametrically opposed to one another, the intent is the same — to be polite.

Having said this, what is considered polite, also, at times, traverses cultures expressing itself congruently in what Nitobe describes as *"little acts scarcely noticeable."* For example, no matter what country you are from, it is common when having a conversation with someone who is standing in the bright sun, for the other person to also position himself in the bright sun to share in their friend's discomfort. This is a sign of sympathetic Politeness that says, *"I will share your discomforts because I care about you."*

Nitobe suggests that some foreigners (i.e. non-Japanese) may slight or snicker at the Japanese elaborate discipline of Politeness — that too much time and energy are invested into the most menial of tasks. However, Nitobe puts forth that *"if there is anything to do, there is certainly a best way to do it, and the best way is both the most economical and the most graceful."*

To me this very much sounds like the purpose behind the Japanese martial arts of Aikido, Iaido, and probably

49

any other martial art. Aren't they the continuous practice of finding the most graceful, efficient way of executing a given technique or sword 'Kata'? Frequently on the mat I hear instructors in our martial arts school say *"Don't have any wasted movement ... Your foot is too far back ... Your posture isn't upright enough ... You're breathing too hard ... Your sword blade is too high ... Now it's too low."* They are all concerned with our efficiency, our economy of movement, our gracefulness, and, therefore, our manners and Politeness.

Of course, this consciousness of Politeness certainly isn't limited to warrior-ship. It can be done with any and every activity. A classic example of this in Japanese culture is the tea ceremony discipline called 'Sado' (or 'Cha-no-yu') where one consciously, deliberately and with absolute, predictable precision manipulates a bowl, a spoon, a napkin, etc. *"To a novice,"* says Nitobe, *"it looks tedious. But one soon discovers that the way prescribed is, after all, the most saving of time and labor; in other words, the most economical use of force, hence ... the most graceful."* In this respect, Politeness actually becomes a powerful spiritual discipline. It is not the activity itself, but the acute mental awareness that is forged within any given discipline that becomes important. *"It is the moral training involved in strict observance of propriety"* that Nitobe emphasizes in this virtue.

Nitobe quotes one of the best (and somewhat controversial) Japanese schools of etiquette for his time, the Ogasawara. *"The end of all etiquette is to so cultivate your mind that even when you are quietly seated, not the roughest ruffian can dare make onset on your person."* I often express this concept to new Aikido and Iaido students when they

Politeness

share concerns or worry about not doing something right, not knowing etiquette, or being afraid of accidentally doing something that might be construed as offensive. *"Your intent is far more important and speaks much louder than any action your make or omit in the 'Dojo',"* I express to them. *"It is your intent which expresses itself through the awareness and integrity of your physical actions. Your specific, physical actions are far less important than the intent we can see behind those actions."* Assertively project your intent to be polite with your posture, gait, facial expressions and other body language, and your actions shall be interpreted as polite.

Politeness can even serve as a remedy to fear. How so? The practice of Politeness (etiquette, manners, or gracefulness) can create states of being that facilitate power, commitment, and even fearless action. Here is a famous Japanese fable called *The Samurai and the Tea Master* that illustrates this notion.

> *A great, but small and frail tea master was walking through the busy streets of Kyoto when he accidentally bumped into the sword of a hot-tempered Samurai. The Samurai, feeling extremely disrespected, demanded that the tea master fight him in a duel. The tea master fervently attempted to apologize to the Samurai explaining that he meant no disrespect, but the Samurai was irate and demanded that they should fight at dawn the next morning at the city gates.*
>
> *The tea master knew that there was no way he could defeat the Samurai, but he also could not dishonor himself or his family by failing to meet in combat. The tea master was terrified. He hurried to the only sword master he knew and pleaded with the sword master to*

train him to become an able swordsman in just one night. The sword master tried, but the tea master was a hopeless student. No matter how patient the sword master was, the tea master remained inept and spiritless.

Feeling unable to help, the sword master said, "Let's take a break. I hear you are a great tea master, would you please make tea for us?"

"Of course," replied the tea master.

As he began his careful, masterfully-practiced preparation of the tea, the sword master's eyes suddenly widened with great enthusiasm. "There! That's it! You must approach your opponent tomorrow in the same spirit you approach your tea ceremonies." With that, the sword master loaned the tea master a 'Katana.'

The following morning, the tea master went to the city gates to meet his fate. Frightened and uncertain of himself, he found that a crowd had gathered, and the Samurai, still fuming with anger, was waiting with his sword drawn. Remembering what the sword master had said, the tea master faced the Samurai on the damp, misty hill. He closed his eyes, set his intention in exactly the same way he did whenever he performed the tea ceremony, accessing the graceful, efficient mastery of his art. Then the tea master slowly lifted his heavy, borrowed sword above his head, and stared into the eyes of his opponent with confidence and composure.

In that moment, the Samurai's face changed from anger to astonishment, and then to humility. The Samurai suddenly threw down his sword, dropped to his knees, and begged the tea master for forgiveness. "Please excuse me, I have been mistaken. Had I known you were such a great swordsman I never would have

Politeness

challenged you! Forgive my short temper and please take me as your student in the tea ceremony so that I may learn to face death with such dignity."

This story illustrates the power of Politeness, the power of gracefulness, the power of efficiency, the power of economy of movement, the power of mastery in all things, in everything and in anything. *"That calmness of mind, that serenity of temper, that composure and quietness of demeanor ... are without doubt the first conditions of right thinking and right feeling,"* says Nitobe. The story of *The Samurai and the Tea Master* exemplifies the composure that comes with well-expressed Politeness. Politeness must, therefore, bear some relationship to Courage as Courage is a product of knowledge and composure. Indeed, the tea master in many respects demonstrated Courage through his mastery of manners, etiquette, and the preparation needed to gracefully execute the actions of his art. Do you see the progression of thought here? Politeness leads to gracefulness. Gracefulness leads to efficiency. Efficiency leads to power. Therefore, couldn't one see how Politeness is a path to power?

Politeness ⇨ Gracefulness ⇨ Efficiency ⇨ Power

I can find no way to state Nitobe's conclusion any better than in his own words, *"... by constant exercise in correct manners [i.e. Politeness], one brings all the parts and faculties of his body into perfect order and into such harmony with itself and its environment as to express the mastery of the spirit over the flesh."* Politeness is a path to power and a

Inner Bushido

means to self-mastery. Does this not sound exactly like the sentiment of Morihei Ueshiba and his explanation of the purpose of Aikido?

The commitment to the proper and perfect exhibition of manners, then, is a direct path for developing power and charisma. Think about someone you know who is powerful and charismatic. Are they polite or rude? Are they graceful or clumsy? Are they attractive or disheveled looking? Is their posture upright and balanced or slouched? The answer to each of these questions is invariably obvious.

We can demonstrate this virtue in any seemingly benign or trivial activity, and perhaps more importantly, we deserve it. We deserve to have the very best drive to work, the very best making of a sandwich for lunch, the very best Aikido workout, or whatever. We can strive to cut our grass with a sense of mastery and grace. We can clean our garage, empty the dishwasher, walk our dogs, or listen to a distressed friend or colleague with that same acute level of awareness that the tea master possessed in his confrontation with the Samurai. Indeed, we can cultivate great power in our lives by striving to practice Politeness, manners, grace, economy, and mastery in everything that we do.

"Fine manners," says Nitobe, *"… mean power in repose."* I interpret this to mean that power is a product of practiced Politeness. Furthermore, *"… a constant practice of graceful deportment must bring with it a reserve and storage of force."* Therefore, one could quite easily conclude that consciously living the Bushido virtue of Politeness actually has the net effect of producing a reserve and storage in the individual (a.k.a. power). Similarly, the

Politeness

practice of martial arts is the pursuit of maximizing one's personal economy of force.

So, is Politeness an antiquated virtue of Bushido? Is there any reason why Politeness cannot exist in our current society as it was espoused in that of feudal Japan? This one is a no-brainer: Absolutely not. Politeness remains powerfully relevant today.

To exhibit Politeness or 'Rei:'

1. **One must possess an acute sense of self-respect manifested initially by his or her physical appearance and secondarily by impeccable social discourse;**
2. **One must strive to execute all of one's tasks and actions with economy and gracefulness, and in turn, stockpile the reserve of power it yields; and**
3. **One must recognize that the path to self-mastery and self-perfection can be pursued through the constant and never-ending efforts at displaying manners.**

In the next chapter on the Bushido virtue of Truthfulness or 'Makoto,' we will explore a topic that has challenged people of all cultures for centuries. We will spend quite some time exploring the relationship between Truthfulness and Politeness from a Bushido perspective. Indeed, we will evaluate the ramifications to husbands around the world of honestly answering common, no-win, catch-22 questions from their wives such as, "Honey, do I look fat in this dress?"

CHAPTER SIX: ONE'S PERFECT WORD

TRUTHFULNESS OR 'MAKOTO'

What can be said about Truthfulness or 'Makoto' (pronounced 'mah-'koh'-'toh')? Can anyone really disagree with its value? Is there any system of values in the world that would object to this virtue? If not, then is this virtue actually unique to Japanese Bushido?

I've really been looking forward to reviewing this virtue for quite some time now. I was expecting it to be an inspiring, insightful portion of the book that would really make me think. The truth is that it did make me think ... a lot. However, this was the first tenet of Nitobe's book that truly disappointed me.

I strongly connect and agree with the importance of the virtue 'Makoto,' but was let down by Nitobe's articulation of the Samurai's use and understanding of the virtue. I'll explain. But before I do, I must also remind the reader that Nitobe is only describing what he believes the Samurai thought of themselves. Nitobe is not necessarily advocating his own opinion, but merely articulating Samurai sentiment. Furthermore, one should remember that Nitobe was not a Samurai, but a Christian academic of the post-Meiji Restoration.

Nitobe attributes near *"transcendental powers"* to the perfection of Truthfulness. Nitobe states, *"Sincerity's far-reaching and long enduring nature is found in its power to produce changes without movement and by its mere presence to accomplish its purpose without effort."* In other words, Truthfulness is self-evident. Truthfulness needs no justification. People can recognize Truthfulness when they see it, hear it, or read it. Truthfulness doesn't need substantiation, an argument or rebuttal. This could also be taken to mean that all one must do is consistently demonstrate Truthfulness for things to work themselves out. This is reminiscent of Taoism's maxim: *"Do nothing and nothing is left undone."* This sentiment could also be similarly stated in the more modern proverbs of *"Always do your best,"* and *"Always be true to yourself."*

Nitobe transitions to Truthfulness from the preceding chapter by again referencing 'Rei' or Politeness by saying that without Truthfulness *"… politeness is a farce and a show."* He introduces the new virtue by citing several epigrams from figures throughout history.

> *"Propriety [appropriate behavior] carried beyond right bounds becomes a lie."*
> — Masamune, Japan's greatest swordsmith (circa. 1300 A.D.)

Truthfulness

"Sincerity is the end and the beginning of all things; without sincerity there would be nothing."
— Tsu-tsu

"Be faithful to thyself: if in your heart you do not stray from truth, the gods will keep you whole."
— An ancient, anonymous poet

These statements provide an excellent contextual starting point for discussion of the 'Makoto' virtue. "Be faithful to *thyself*." Notice that this poet did not say, "Be faithful to *your lord*." Nitobe cites this ancient, anonymous poet, but fails to emphasize the quote's importance. In feudal Japan, being faithful to thyself was rarely espoused, but instead being faithful to a lord was thought of as virtuous. This is a shame because I think the Samurai would probably have survived had they had paid more attention to the lesson in this quote. The problem with committing your life solely to the service of others, rather than also living for oneself, is that when you live only for others, who will be there to take care of you? Eventually, you prematurely expire in one way or another, as the Samurai did.

Nitobe states that lying and equivocation (a statement that is not literally false but that cleverly avoids an unpleasant truth) were deemed cowardly by the Samurai. Furthermore, he states that the high social position of the Samurai *"demanded a loftier standard of truthfulness than that of the tradesman and peasant."* Here is where I must first take issue with this Samurai attitude because to me it hints of arrogance. In my opinion, especially today, one's degree of expressing Truthfulness should have absolutely nothing to do with one's social position or class. There is absolutely no reason at all why a 'Bushi's degree of Truthfulness should be held to a higher or lower standard than that of anyone else from another social class such as a tradesman or peasant. Furthermore, I am rather disappointed at the not-so-subtle, underlying assumption that a Samurai was superior to any other class. I find this even more disturbing in that although *humility* is another frequently stated attribute of a Samurai's character, I fail to sense any humility in the statement or belief that perceives one's social status, and its subsequent moral/ethical responsibility, as superior to another.

Although Nitobe claims that lying and equivocation were deemed cowardly by the Samurai, I have observed (with quite a bit of frequency I'm afraid) far too much equivocation and, for lack of a better description, "less that complete truthfulness" when disagreement occurs in martial arts communities. Frequently, people will pretend to take the high road and inject into the disagreement ill-defined, ambiguous terms like 'Budo' and 'Giri' along with other vague, conveniently-malleable words and concepts to attempt to justify and rationalize their inappropriate actions. Similarly, such individuals sometimes point to others and make opposing public claims such as, *"He is not acting in accordance with Bushido, but I am! I'm right and he is wrong! I'm ethical, and he is not! I'm good and he is bad!"* Indeed, these individuals use their inadequate and vague understanding of Bushido as a feeble shield to hide behind. Many of those with only a neophyte understanding of Bushido are completely unaware of the fact that there is no formal or official

Truthfulness

declaration of what Bushido is or is not. Therefore, how can one claim that someone else is not acting in accordance with it?

This is a sad phenomenon. Just because people disagree doesn't mean that one person has to be right and the other person wrong. Just because people disagree doesn't mean that one person is good and one is bad ... that one person is moral and the other is immoral ... ethical or unethical. Just because people disagree at times doesn't necessarily mean that one person is acting in accordance with Bushido and the other is not.

The next area of contention that disappointed me surrounded 'Bushido no ichi-gon' or "the word of a Samurai." The Chinese 'Kanji' or ideogram used in Japanese language for Truthfulness is a combination of "word" and "perfect." So, 'Makoto' or Truthfulness can be read as one's "perfect word." According to Nitobe, the word of a Samurai was considered sufficient guarantee of Truthfulness and any request for a written pledge of Truthfulness was considered offensive and beneath his dignity. I find this assertion both silly and contradictory. The *written* word for Truthfulness is "perfect word," yet a Samurai would be offended at the suggestion of being asked to put their "perfect word" in writing? This is non-rational.

It seems to me that someone who claims to follow Bushido and claims to exhibit the virtue of Truthfulness wouldn't have a problem with, and may possibly even be proud to put their "perfect word" in writing. If a 'Bushi' really intends to be truthful and honest, then he or she should not object to a physical symbol of their virtue such as being willing to put their "perfect word" in writing. If those who claim to practice Bushido were more willing to put their "perfect word" in writing, there would be less room for disagreement and it would be far more apparent when one person was acting in accordance with their "perfect word" and when another was not. Doesn't that make sense?

Assuming a Samurai was literate — and it is very likely that many were not — there is only one reason alleged followers of Bushido would refuse to commit their "perfect word" in writing and it has nothing to do with Honor, Respect, or Politeness. The reason for their objection is that the person has no intention of honoring their "perfect word." Or, one only has the intention of honoring their word, if convenient. Indeed, they have an ulterior motive. They want wiggle room to go back on their "perfect word." They want the ability to maneuver their way with various degrees of verbal equivocation to fabricate whatever conclusion they want at the time of or subsequent to a disagreement. They want the creative license to spontaneously edit their verbal commitments, to re-justify their actions, so that ultimately, they can convince themselves and others into believing that they are acting ethically. This technique allows them to live with their dishonesty on a day-to-day basis.

I find the Samurai's unwillingness to put their oral pledges in writing a considerable contradiction. It seems that many Samurai were content, even proud, to literally "seal with blood" their pledge. Is not sealing an agreement with blood as comparably symbolic and physical a gesture as a written pledge? Why is this gesture not considered beneath a Samurai's dignity? Why would a Samurai be willing to seal their pledge with blood, but not in written word? If you can divorce your mind for just a moment of any preconceived illusions about the Samurai or their alleged virtues, the answer becomes obvious: When you seal an agreement only with blood, one can easily challenge, object to, and change after the fact what *exactly* was pledged in blood. One can claim disagreement over the nature and terms of the original agreement. They can then use this ambiguity to justify a new course of action that is askew from their previous commitment.

Disagreements like this usually sound like, *"I didn't agree to that! What I agreed to was something different."* "Oh, no," says the other party. *"That's not true. I remember it very clearly. What you agreed to was ..."* *"Well, yes, maybe that is partly correct, but that was only if ... "* You see? Do you see the problems that vague oral commitments can lead to?

Written agreements virtually eliminate this equivocating "escape route" — this rationalization process. Written agreements keep people more honest and make it very clear what was and what was not agreed to – or, at least makes it much more evident as to when someone is or is not honoring their perfect word. To me, nothing could be more honest, more mature, and representative of one's "perfect word," and more consistent with Bushido's virtue of Truthfulness than a written agreement.

Some may continue to assert that a physical symbol shouldn't be necessary of a 'Bushi'; and I shall continue to challenge this. Based on the admittedly modest amount of information I have exposed myself to about Samurai history, there's an abundance of accounts describing warring Samurai factions all claiming to uphold the virtues of Bushido, fighting one another over a disagreement of commitment with another Samurai or clan. This is not all that different from religious wars where each party claims to have God on their side. Perhaps if there were a mutually-created, physical symbol (something more tangible than just their so-called "perfect word") representing the details of an oral agreement, for example, a written document, there would be less question as to whether a Samurai was living up to their virtue of Truthfulness, or not.

In my opinion, the unwillingness of a Samurai or one claiming to follow Bushido to put one's perfect word in writing, if asked for, is the epitome of cowardice – the very opposite of Courage. Therefore, the virtue of Courage must precede the virtue of Truthfulness because it can take Courage to be truthful. A true practitioner of Bushido wouldn't object to a written pledge, but instead would revel in it. When I read of Nitobe's assertion that *"the best of Samurai looked upon an oath as derogatory to their honor,"* all I can think of is Hamlet's, *"The lady doth protest too much."* In my opinion, this is little more than a thinly-veiled, pseudo-intellectual attempt to redirect one's attention away from the real issue at hand, which is that the person doesn't really have the intention to heed their word.

Nitobe then goes on to state *"A recent American writer,"* referencing Dr. R.B. Peery, author of *The Gist of Japan*, 1897, *"is responsible for the statement: If you ask an ordinary Japanese which is better, to tell a falsehood or be impolite, he will not hesitate to answer 'to tell a falsehood!'"* In other words, Dr. Peery is suggesting that the Japanese people of the 1800s think it is better to lie than to be impolite. Nitobe argues that this is too strong a statement, saying that this is no different than a Westerner who tells a pleasant and convenient white lie when he responds, *"I feel well,"* even if he actually feels sick to his stomach. I concur with Nitobe that social etiquette of any culture is full of these minor falsehoods and that it is acceptable to engage in such — the reason being that there is no real *intention* to deceive, but merely to be polite and not inconvenience another person with an unnecessary unpleasantry such as, *"I have bad gas. Thank you for asking."* Although this is a literal falsehood or 'Uso,' this is not the kind of dishonesty that Bushido regarded as unacceptable. I have seen countless times in martial arts programs students who get hurt or tired, then are subsequently asked whether or not they are hurt or tired, to which the sore, exhausted students promptly answer, "No, Sensei." There is nothing wrong with this kind of falsehood. This brings up the importance of making a distinction between truth ('Makoto') and fact ('Honto'). It is clear that Bushido emphasizes the importance of espousing truth, rather than literal fact. This is not equivocation because the intent of equivocating is deception in most cases, which does not apply here.

All systems of philosophy are artificial and, subsequently, fallible. Therefore, to function effectively and harmoniously in society one must be mentally-pliant and willing to function outside of the literal canon of any given system of values, including Bushido. For example, let's say a rather unkempt, anxious, and angry-looking person with a gun in their hand knocks on the door one afternoon and says, "Do you know where I can find your brother?" Would an advocate of Bushido truthfully assist this person? Or might it be best to tell a falsehood? Clearly this would be equivocating, for my intent is to deceive the individual at the door. However, isn't my deception appropriate? In this case, being a Bushido "fundamentalist" would be destructive. That is why we must never abandon our rational responsibilities of adulthood to a philosophical ideal. There are times when deception is appropriate, even admirable, but this indeed is a slippery slope.

With this awareness one must also come to recognize that "truth" is a relative term and that multiple truths, and often seemingly contradictory truths, can exist simultaneously. Multiple truths exist because every person has his own vantage point and perspective. What appears true to one person from one perspective may seem false to another. Where disagreement occurs is when one person selfishly fails to accept the reality that others are allowed to feel, think, see, and value things differently from oneself or when one or both parties fail to reveal their true intentions in a given relationship.

> *"Selfishness is not living as one wishes to live,*
> *it is asking others to live as one wishes to live."*
> — Oscar Wilde (1854-1900), Irish Writer

When I was a very young man, a senior student I looked up to or 'Sempai' of mine, who rather serendipitously was then exactly the age I am now at the time of this writing, told me that if I insist on holding other people to the same standards I hold for myself, I would be consistently disappointed and very unhappy in life. He was very wise and I have found his words to be very true. Since then, I have attempted to pass on that same sentiment to others.

In my experience, those who insist on other people seeing things exactly the way that they do themselves, are

Truthfulness

constantly disappointed, frustrated and angry people. The origin of these adverse feelings is conceit and arrogance or even more fundamentally, insecurity in themselves. For, if one is truly secure in his own sense of truth, beliefs, and opinions, then he is not threatened by those who have their own standards, truths, and opinions.

Although it doesn't relate directly to the virtue being discussed, I was further disappointed by what I detected as an attitude of nationalistic conceit that Nitobe seems to express in this Truthfulness essay. For example, when exploring the difference, if any, between truth and fact, Nitobe begins his articulation with, *"Ask a Japanese, or even an American of any refinement ..."* The not-so-subtle implication being made here is that Japanese are superior to Americans, specifically those Americans *"of any refinement."* By today's standards of political correctness and even the most fundamental bar of social etiquette, a statement of this kind was unnecessary even in 1899. Furthermore, such a drastic failure of social etiquette on the part of Nitobe himself, rather ironically, may have demonstrated the opposite of his very own assertion. It seems no one is immune from demonstrating arrogance, conceit, and prejudice. I do not exempt myself from this possibility either. We are all just human, which, almost by definition, means that we are all flawed and fail to demonstrate our highest selves at times.

Nitobe now does something that I found quite unexpected and unusual in the chapter. He turns his attention for a rather surprising amount of time to the subject of Bushido's virtue of Truthfulness as it relates to business ethics and commerce. It is in this portion of the chapter that I became further disappointed in Nitobe's analysis. In his digression, Nitobe clearly takes this opportunity to interject his own, personal beliefs about commerce ethics into the discussion. Personally, I find his assessment to be highly-flawed. Since this digression is not necessarily central or of interest to a reader of this chapter I shall simply move on. However, if you are curious about Nitobe's thoughts on how Bushido's sense of 'Makoto' relates to commerce and business ethics, please reference the bonus chapter of this book where I shall make my analysis on this subject available.

At this point, I think it would be valuable to restate the quote from the anonymous poet cited earlier: *"Be faithful to thyself: if in your heart you do not stray from truth, the gods will keep you whole."* In today's post-feudal world where people live for themselves and their families and not for a "lord" of any context, I think one's sense and understanding of Bushido must become more self-concentric. This awareness requires a level of internal honesty that must take precedence over any commitment to an external authority figure such as an employer, leader, and even a martial arts teacher. It does not mean that one can't or shouldn't exhibit Respect, Honor, and Loyalty to an external authority figure, when appropriate. It simply means one should not be mindlessly respectful, mindlessly honorable or mindlessly loyal.

So, is 'Makoto' antiquated? Absolutely not. However, a mature perspective must at the very least recognize that truth is different than fact; and while fact could be argued to be absolute (although I think a formidable argument could also be made that fact is even relative), truth is often a concept relative to the one perceiving an event, situation or circumstance. We must carry our own truth

Truthfulness

within us. When we are quiet, still, non-judgmental and honest with ourselves, we can quickly and accurately ascertain whether or not something we think or believe about ourselves is truthful or not.

In summary:

1. **Truthfulness is self-evident, needs no justification and can produce change by its mere presence;**
2. **Truthfulness requires being faithful to oneself first; and**
3. **Truthfulness means being willing to put your "perfect word" in writing if asked for.**

According to Nitobe, Honesty is intimately blended in its etymology with Honor. Therefore, Honor will be the subject of our next chapter.

CHAPTER SEVEN: SELF-RESPECT

HONOR OR ′MEIYO′

Honor or 'Meiyo' (pronounced 'meh'-'ee'-'yoh') is a concept that carries significant weight in any culture. It is a concept that most people think they should value, but perhaps have never really explored its meaning and significance and often take its use in everyday language for granted. Many believe that it is important to "honor" parents, elders, and people of authority; and most of us appreciate being "honored" by others for an achievement such as a graduation, award, long-term commitment, or contribution to society. It seems clear that most people would agree that Honor is an important virtue. However, when asked to define Honor, many people struggle.

How is Honor differentiated from Respect, Politeness, or deference? Is there any distinction between these concepts? How do you know when you have achieved an honorable status? Is Honor something that is bestowed upon you by others? Just because you are honored by others, does that make you right, ethical, or moral? Does Honor really matter? People often think it is virtuous to fight for their Honor or the Honor of a loved one — in some cases willing to fight to the death. As such, it has always seemed strange to me that cultures would so strongly value something that was so ill-defined. How can something so prized by societies be so ambiguous?

An encyclopedia defines Honor as *"the evaluation of a person's social status as judged by that individual's community."* I think many people, if not most, would agree with the crux of this definition. However, this definition lacks any checks and balances of whether or not one *should* be honored. For example, Adolf Hitler was honored by his community. Did this kind of consensus by his peers and fellow citizens make him honorable? I think most would readily say, no.

Far too often, people abuse the concept of Honor, unfairly labeling whomever they might adamantly disagree with as "dishonorable." Rather than simply be content to agree to disagree, they sometimes feel compelled to demonize and vilify a person who might simply share a different opinion or different set of values. I have seen this occur repeatedly in martial arts communities where one person (usually a teacher) either claims to have been "dishonored" by another teacher, peer, or even a student. Or, a person points the finger at someone they disagree with and publicly campaigns against that person to be thought by their community as dishonorable and "not behaving in accordance with Bushido." Sometimes they are actually just hiding behind their own poorly-developed sense of Honor, representing little more than a transparent effort to camouflage or ignore their own insecurities. I call this effort "playing the Bushido card." It is essentially the equivalent of a church labeling anything they don't understand or don't agree with as "the work of the devil." Whatever its incarnation, it is an unacceptable human behavior that must be nipped in the bud.

Many people believe Honor carries with it additional meaning and responsibilities in a martial arts context (although I'm not certain this belief is true). Martial arts students know that they are expected to always Honor their teachers. But what *exactly* does this mean? What does it equate to in terms of action? And, are there limits to this kind of Honor? In light of these ambiguities, we shall carefully explore Nitobe's work in hopes it can offer some direction in better understanding the notion of Honor. Honor or 'Meiyo' is the most enigmatic of the seven virtues of Bushido articulated by Nitobe and, therefore, is also the virtue most susceptible to misinterpretation and abuse.

What I found in this chapter of Nitobe's treatise on Honor was largely what I reluctantly expected I would find: that in all likelihood the historical Samurai did not live up to the philosophical height and the near-mythological spirit assigned to them, which is often revered by those in the martial arts, the corporate business world, and other communities today. I was not disappointment in Nitobe, but of what he reports the Samurai's practice of Honor was. I very much value what Nitobe professes Honor *should* be. However, he sadly reports that the actual practice of Honor — as it relates to historical Bushido — was, far too often, rare among the Samurai class.

While disappointed, I certainly wasn't surprised by any means. I had no illusions that Samurai would be the one cultural icon that actually did live up to its lore. However, I can think of no other way to most concisely describe what the Samurai insisted Honor was other than: egotism. Thankfully, Nitobe successfully rehabilitates the reputation of the Samurai and their so-called virtue of Honor from that of childish egotism to that of mature wisdom. Once again, I feel compelled to remind readers that Nitobe is only describing what he understands the Samurai's sense of Honor to have been, and that he is not necessarily condoning their position. In this chapter I was reassured by Nitobe's own personal interjections that redeem the majority of the chapter's disappointing content and Nitobe, for lack of a better description, scolds the immature articulation of Honor that feudal Bushido allegedly espoused. Instead, Nitobe offers a far more evolved and wise interpretation of what the precept of Honor should be as an ideal rather than the way it was, no doubt, practiced and exercised in reality.

Nitobe acknowledges that one of the greatest challenges surrounding the concept of Honor is that there is no clear definition of what Honor really is. Such did not exist during the Samurai's reign, during the Meiji restoration, and, one could argue, not even now to a great extent. *"It was a great pity that nothing clear and general was expressed as to what constitutes Honor,"* Nitobe states. However, he then offers a powerfully succinct definition: Honor is *"a vivid consciousness of personal dignity."* This is a good starting point for discussion.

A *"vivid consciousness"* implies one's own *self*-perception. Notice that Nitobe did not say a vivid *reputation*, which would imply a *collective* perception of a person in the eyes of others. Use of the word consciousness suggests that Honor is a *self*-ascribed determination, one that has absolutely nothing to do with outside influence or the opinions of others. Therefore, Honor is what you think of yourself, though not always and not necessarily what you show others in public. And, more importantly, Honor is *not* rooted in what other people think of you. In direct contradiction to many definitions of the word, Honor is not necessarily defined by your reputation. Honor is something you carry inside yourself, not something others assign to you. However, if asked in a survey, I'm certain a high percentage of respondents would define some element of Honor as involving the collective impressions of one's peers or community.

Use of the adjective *"vivid"* I think was also carefully chosen by Nitobe. Vivid means clear, strong, and/or graphic. Therefore, possessing Honor requires more than just a vague consciousness or awareness of oneself. Honor requires a clear, strong, and graphic sense of self. The vividness of Honor implies that the ultimate "source" of Honor lies within. It is an immortal part of oneself. Nitobe's definition also includes the words *"personal"* and *"dignity."* Use of the word *"personal"* further delineates the quality of independence inherent within the virtue of Honor, eliminating outside influence — the opinions, gossip, or actions of others. Dignity has been defined as *"the quality of being worthy of esteem or respect"* and since we are talking about *"personal dignity"* we are, in fact, talking about personal respect or self-respect. Perhaps then, I could offer an even more concise definition suggesting that Honor is, in its simplest form, self-respect. As such, it must be recognized before we proceed further that Honor is completely, one-hundred percent within the control of each individual. Honor has absolutely nothing to do with what someone else says or thinks of you.

> *"Honor is what no man can give you –*
> *and none can take away.*
> *Honor is the gift a man gives himself."*
> — Liam Neeson, portraying Scottish folk hero,
> *Rob Roy*, in the 1995 film

However, how many times in pop-culture media have protagonists or antagonists claimed to have been dishonored by someone else? How many dozens of movies (either American or Japanese) are based on the idea of winning back one's Honor? And, how often do people in these movies and even in real life use the word "Honor" merely as a substitute for the more honest and often more embarrassing, truthful term of "ego?" Use of Nitobe's excellent definition of Honor, of course, makes such a means to dishonor impossible since others cannot inflict or assign dishonor upon you.

In an age of excessive political correctness, people often try to simply change one's *vocabulary* instead of trying to change one's *behavior*. For example, rather than acknowledge to oneself that he is "fat," a person

Honor

often chooses to describe himself as "overweight," "big-boned" or "husky." This is a weak effort to talk oneself out of having to change or take action. It is far easier to simply change the *word* fat to overweight than it is to change the *behaviors* that make one fat. Similarly, rather than work on evolving one's self-respect and/or humility, people today will often use the word "Honor" when, in reality, they are just referring to their ego. Using the word "Honor" sounds much more mature and prestigious than acknowledging one's ego has run amuck. However, simply changing the vocabulary one uses to describe oneself does not actually equate to a change in the person's behavior or character. Nitobe offers a thoughtful, perceptive analysis of Honor that can assist someone truly wanting to transcend their shallow egotism to that of deep Honor.

An excellent and fairly contemporary pop-culture example (or some might say "classic" depending on one's age) of this common and juvenile misunderstanding of Honor is illustrated in the 1985 martial arts movie, *The Karate Kid: Part Two*. In that story, a spoiled local boy from a prominent Okinawan family is inadvertently, but publicly, exposed and humiliated for cheating the townspeople out of the fair trade of goods by the movie's protagonist. The disgraced young man subsequently blames the movie's hero for "dishonoring" him and predictably vows retribution. Now, certainly, this storyline is plainly transparent. The young man wasn't dishonored by the movie's hero. The young man dishonored himself by engaging in the dishonest behavior to begin with. However, we see this theme repeated in hundreds of stories throughout recorded history. Unfortunately, many people in real life don't learn the lesson no matter how many incarnations they are exposed to. That lesson being: Only you can dishonor yourself. Certainly, Samurai (being ordinary human beings, not super-men) were as susceptible to this experience as any other.

Immediately after proposing his definition of Honor, Nitobe then offers a caveat of sorts that *"any infringement upon [Honor's] integrity was felt as shame"* not just by Samurai, but by all Japanese. The Japanese seem to hold in esteem the value of shame. This value appears to be a driving force behind Honor and other virtues such as Politeness and Loyalty. A sense of shame or 'Ren-chi-shin' was (and still is) instilled in Japanese children at a very young age. *"Indeed, the sense of shame seems to me to be the earliest indication of the moral consciousness of our race,"* says Nitobe. He further emphasizes this Japanese sentiment by citing Scottish satirical writer and controversial social commentator, Thomas Carlyle (1795-1881), who says that *"shame is the soil of all Virtue, of good manners and good morals."*

Thus far, I have no objection to Nitobe's monologue of shame and the relationship that shame bears to Honor. However, it is at this point that I offer what I think is an important distinction that Nitobe hints at but fails to emphasize. The source of shame or the source of Honor is critically important and I think here it is being glossed over. It is the *source* of shame or Honor that differentiates the virtue of true Honor from that of simple egotism.

Based solely on Nitobe's work, the Japanese society that Nitobe speaks of seems to fail to make the distinction between what could be termed as internally-catalyzed shame and externally-catalyzed shame; internally-catalyzed Honor and externally-catalyzed Honor.

In other words,

- **No one can shame you, only you can shame you.**
- **No one can dishonor you, only you can dishonor you.**
- **If you perceive yourself as shamed by someone else (i.e. "He shamed me."), your motivation is egotism.**
- **If you perceive yourself as dishonored by someone else (i.e. "He dishonored me."), your motivation is egotism.**

For example, let's say an adult first-born son engages in a crime and is sentenced to jail. One might be inclined, whether Japanese or not, to feel that the son has shamed the whole family. However, I disagree. The son has shamed only himself, and has brought dishonor to himself, but to suggest that his action shames and dishonors the whole family is nothing more than cowardly narcissism. Remember, Honor is a vivid consciousness of personal dignity. A family is not in control of, and therefore, is not responsible for the actions of any grown member of that family.

As a second, more subtle dynamic of Honor, Nitobe praises the historical reputation of Iyeyasu (pronounced 'ee'-'yeh'-'yah'-'soo'), the first 'Shogun' of the Tokugawa period of feudal Japan (circa 1600 - 1616 A.D.). Nitobe asserts Iyeyasu to be a man who practiced what he preached and exemplified the true, non-egotistical virtue of Honor and its inherent qualities contained therein of

Inner Bushido

patience, forbearance, and countenance. Nitobe's praise of Iyeyasu came in the form of citing an un-named contemporary who wrote of the 'Shogun' in comparison to other past Japanese leaders of the Tokugawa period:

- **To Nobunaga he attributed,** *"I will kill her, if the nightingale sings not in time;"*
- **To Hideyoshi he attributed,** *"I will force her to sing for me;"* and
- **To Iyeyasu he attributed,** *"I will wait till she opens her lips."*

If this attribution to Iyeyasu is historically accurate and fairly representative of his reign, then I think it is wonderful that Nitobe references Iyeyasu as one who truly exemplified Honor's qualities of patience and forbearance.

Nitobe quotes, but does not necessarily condone, the statement of another anonymous contemporary, *"That Samurai was right who refused to compromise his character by a slight humiliation in his youth ... because ... dishonor is like a scar on a tree, which, instead of effacing, only helps to enlarge."* By mature, Western values, does this not sound like pure, unadulterated egotism, arrogance, and vanity? Is this an example of the precept of Japanese knighthood that we are to follow? If so, then I must reconsider my desire to follow so-called Bushido.

Nitobe then continues his rehabilitation of this virtue by chiding an all too common occurrence within the Samurai's so-called exercising of Bushido's Honor. *"In the name of Honor, deeds were perpetrated which can find no justification in the code of Bushido. At the slightest, even imaginary insult, the quick-tempered braggart took offense, resorted to the use of the sword, and many an unnecessary strife was raised and many innocent lives lost."* I was relieved to read that Nitobe recognizes the confusion between Honor and ego. Nitobe continues, *"Honor [was] too often nothing higher than vain glory or worldly approval ..."* and *"[F]or the most part, an insult was quickly resented and repaid by death."* If this is true, it further suggests that many 'Bushi' failed to exercise true Honor and also failed to demonstrate the virtue of Benevolence discussed in a previous chapter.

A true 'Bushi,' a real follower of Bushido, would, of course, simply ignore a slight insult (or even a significant one, for that matter). Unfortunately, I think far too many neophyte followers of Bushido today (even those who may hold high-ranking black belts in martial arts) fail to make this distinction and unconsciously perceive the terms Honor and ego as synonyms for each other. Far too many in the martial arts communities take offense too quickly to miscommunications, demonstrate far too little desire to be patient and prudent, to have respect for those who may have different opinions than others, to investigate one's motive, fact-find, and ask for clarification before taking offense and drawing their metaphoric sword.

It is my opinion that there should be an inverse relationship between one's rank and one's tendency to take offense. That is to say, the higher one's rank in martial arts is, the more difficult it should be to offend that person. High-ranking black belts should develop "thicker skin," not become more psychologically fragile and entitlement-privy with the ascension of one's rank. However, this has not been my observation of many (though certainly not all) in some martial arts communities.

Inner Bushido

Nitobe describes the Samurai's sense of Honor as *"extreme sensitiveness"* and *"the delicate code of Honor."* Honor, a vivid consciousness of personal dignity, as Nitobe suggests, should be strong, stable, and relatively unshakable — not delicate and sensitive. The mere assertion that the Samurai's sense of Honor was *"extremely sensitive"* or *"delicate"* as Nitobe states, suggests that far too often Samurai acted like insecure juveniles lacking any real practice or demonstration of Honor. If they really possessed Honor, slight provocation and/or offense wouldn't lead to quick-tempered violence that Nitobe states was far too routine. I was pleased to see Nitobe's disapproval of such behavior: *"To take offense at slight provocation was ridiculed as 'short-tempered.'"*

A person of real Bushido would never fatally strike down another for a slight humiliation or insult of any kind. Instead, a true follower of Bushido would consider following a precept of Chinese philosopher Mencius who said, *"Though you bare yourself and insult me, what is that to me? You cannot taint my soul by your outrage."* This reminds me of the title and fundamental message of a 1979 book by Dr. Terry Cole-Whittaker that I often reference: *What You Think of Me Is None of My Business.* Mencius also taught that *"anger at a petty offense is unworthy of a superior man ..."* Nitobe quickly follows this advice with the acknowledgement that *"very few Bushi attained this sublime height of magnanimity, patience, and forgiveness."* This is the ideal response and behavior of a 'Bushi' that Nitobe reluctantly acknowledges was rare. In other words, the overwhelming majority of Samurai did not consistently live up to the precept of Honor. Some might suggest that not much has changed over the centuries, except that instead of immediately exercising a Samurai's right to execute offenders, modern day martial artists are simply censured, ostracized, or excommunicated. Of course, though, this is certainly progress.

To further demonstrate the abuse of this virtue in this context of Samurai culture, Nitobe states that fame, and not wealth or knowledge, was the goal toward which youths had to strive. Parents even seemed to endorse this effort. Nitobe cites *"[M]any an ambitious mother refused to see her sons again unless they could 'return home,' ... 'caparisoned in brocade' [richly ornamented in reputational success]."* Nitobe also states that Samurai boys *"... knew that Honor won in youth grows with age."* To me, this is all very disappointing. Perhaps I am disappointed because I am from a Western country and am of Western values. I was raised to recognize that fame for the sake of fame was not virtuous. After all, isn't that how we ended up with socialite tabloid celebrities who appear to be famous for no apparent reason beyond their public, video-recorded sexual escapades? Almost by definition, the notion of fame itself is inherently wrapped up in one's reputation being determined and sustained by what others think. This would be the anti-thesis of Nitobe's suggestion that Honor is a vivid consciousness of personal dignity.

Furthermore, I think to myself, if I were a parent, would I encourage my children to strive for fame over wealth and knowledge? Certainly, not. In my opinion, this would be a failure of my fiduciary as a parent. Again, if this representation of Honor is that which I am required to abide by to be a practitioner of Bushido, then I, once again, would like no part of it. I am, on the other hand, very interested in being a disciple of the virtue that Nitobe endorses, which, in my opinion, is the true gravitational center of modern Bushido, not that of historical Samurai folklore.

As I have concluded in the previous chapters exploring Bushido's virtues, Bushido is not antiquated, nor is its virtue of Honor. Quite to the contrary, Honor is a key element of Bushido's infrastructure of both the past and present. However, I'm afraid that a true understanding of Honor (that which Nitobe articulates) is not the colloquial understanding of Honor today. Too many people, including some martial arts students and martial arts teachers, confuse the source of real Honor, that being a *"vivid consciousness of personal dignity,"* and instead erroneously utilize the term Honor as a synonym for ego or reputation. Nothing could be further from the truth.

In this chapter, Nitobe is conceding that Bushido was not a carefully followed system of values by the majority of Samurai during their era. Instead, Bushido is a conceptual philosophy, a near-mythological ideal that has been historically and artificially "rehabilitated" by those such as Nitobe (and others) in times since and even before the official "decommissioning" of the Samurai.

Much like the Christians' Jesus probably didn't actually walk on water, a young George Washington probably didn't actually chop down a cherry tree, and Tombstone's Wyatt Earp may not have been as tough and virtuous as he is often portrayed in film, the Samurai as a collective class probably didn't actually live by this unwritten, ambiguous, and conveniently-malleable "code of conduct" the way we idolize them in Hollywood movies, cultural fables, fictional novels, and martial arts schools of today. However, that doesn't in any way diminish the value of Bushido as it is and should be understood and practiced.

I left this chapter concluding in congruence with the impressions made upon me by earlier chapters and virtues that Nitobe, a Christian academic, was, at least intellectually, more Samurai than those who actually were of the Samurai class. Were it within my power to do so, I would posthumously bestow upon Inazo Nitobe an honorary designation of Samurai, for in this chapter Nitobe successfully rehabilitates the historical Samurai of feudal Japan to the ideal of modern Bushido.

In the next chapter, we will explore the seventh of these seven virtues of Bushido: Loyalty. This, too, I'm afraid may be another virtue marred by well-intentioned, but overly pop-culture-influenced Bushido enthusiasts — many of whom reside in the martial arts community.

We can practice Honor by recognizing that:

1. **Honor is a vivid consciousness of personal dignity so strong that it doesn't require defending;**
2. **Honor is self-respect; it is something you give yourself; and cannot be taken away from you without your consent; and**
3. **Honor is not rooted in your communal reputation; and is not defined or designated by others.**

CHAPTER EIGHT: LISTENING TO ONE'S HIGHEST SELF

LOYALTY OR 'CHUUGI'

At last we reach the final virtue of Bushido: Loyalty or 'Chuugi' (pronounced 'choo'-'ghee'). Oh, how I've long awaited to explore this virtue. I really expected this to be a prominent section in Nitobe's book. However, surprisingly, his Loyalty monologue is the most brief of the seven virtues even though he purports *"… it is only in the code of chivalrous Honor that Loyalty assumes paramount importance."* This would certainly explain why Loyalty comes last in the discussion, but it doesn't explain the brevity. Nitobe takes a somewhat disappointing, "It is what it is" approach to explaining this virtue and this is the first and only virtue that he doesn't challenge or

Inner Bushido

attempt to rehabilitate. One is led to conclude that he finds nothing to object to. He doesn't outright endorse the Samurai perspective, but simultaneously, he doesn't seem to feel offended or embarrassed by the notion as he clearly did with other virtues such as Honor, Courage, and Benevolence. Due to Nitobe's brevity on the subject, I have heavily consulted other academics to help explore the various definitions, characteristics and dynamics of this very important virtue.

In stark contrast to the introduction of previous virtues, Nitobe offers no formal definition of Loyalty, but instead offers fleeting descriptors such as *"[Paying] homage and fealty to a superior is a distinct feature of Bushido's Loyalty."* He also offers that *"Loyalty is the keystone of the feudal virtues making a symmetrical arch."*

Nitobe assumes that his audience already understands the word and, instead, spends most of this article

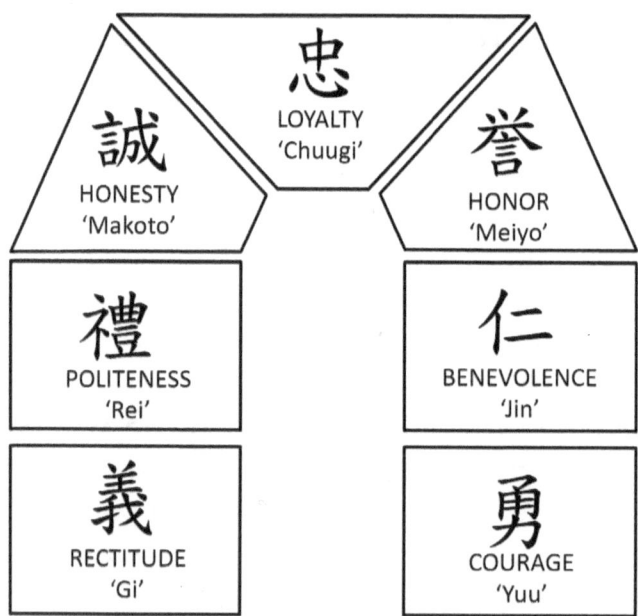

Loyalty

discussing the differences in the cultural application of Loyalty, primarily comparing Japanese to Western values. I found this valuable, but also inadequate. I would argue that a lack of consensus about what Loyalty is contributes to the present day misuse and abuse of this virtue, particularly in the context of some martial arts communities.

Although today's scholars greatly disagree with one another's proposed definitions of Loyalty, Loyalty can be generically defined as faithfulness or devotion to a person, country, group, cause, or idea. However, I tend to concur with philosophy professors John Ladd and Marcia Baron, of Brown University and Indiana University respectively, who both characterize Loyalty as relating solely to an inter-personal relationship. That is, you can be loyal only to another person, but not to an inanimate object, cause, or idea. *"When we speak of causes (or ideals) we are more apt to say that people are committed to them or devoted to them than that they are loyal to them,"* says Baron. Loyalty suggests people-to-people connections, not so much people-to-ideals. For sake of simplicity, our discussions in this chapter will initially be limited to this inter-personal definition of Loyalty before proposing an intra-personal definition of Loyalty. Also, at this time, we will only briefly mention any relationship Loyalty may have to patriotism even though as we discussed early in this book that Bushido is closely related to the concept of patriotism.

Nitobe attempts to clarify and distinguish Bushido's Loyalty from a Western audience's sense of Loyalty by offering the following comparison. *"In America where 'everybody is as good as anybody, else' ... such exalted ideas*

Inner Bushido

of Loyalty as we [Japanese] feel for our sovereign may be deemed 'excellent within certain bounds,' but preposterous as encouraged among us [Japanese]." Also, he offers, *"... Loyalty as we [Japanese] conceive it may find few admirers elsewhere, not because our conception is wrong, but because it is forgotten, and also because we carry it to a degree not reached in any other country."*

Nitobe then educates his readers to an earlier century's sense of Japanese Loyalty with an appalling story about a set of parents who deliberately participate in a ruse, beheading their own innocent child to save the life of their lord's child. He attempts to compose the hopefully false story's atrocity by likening it to the Christian biblical story of Abraham's intent to sacrifice his son, Isaac. However, a problem with this comparison is that both stories are equally disgusting. Nitobe states that *"in both cases it was obedience to the call of duty, utter submission to the command of a higher voice."* I find this rationalization childish. The higher calling that both the parents of the young Japanese boy and Abraham should have listened to was their own higher-self calling, a voice of reason and rationality ... in a word ... Rectitude.

Nitobe further attempts to illustrate Japanese Loyalty in comparison to Western values by adding, *"The individualism of the West, which recognizes separate interests for father and son, husband and wife, necessarily brings into strong relief the duties owed by one to the other; but Bushido held that the interest of the family and the members thereof is intact — one and inseparable."* This is certainly a key cultural distinction that accounts for why Western audiences might pigeon hole the Japanese sense of Loyalty as excessive or extreme. Conversely, it explains why a Japanese audience might describe Western Loyalty as weak, relative, or conditional. Being of Western culture, I choose to reject the feudal Japanese sense of Loyalty because I was born and raised in a culture that promotes individualism as one of its highest values; and after many years of careful self-exploration and study, I continue to agree with the integrity of that value. Whereas, historically there exists a trend that Japanese culture de-emphasizes a sense of individualism and instead emphasizes a sense of conformity. However, my understanding is that this, too, is presently changing in Japan — perhaps because this is more natural and intuitive to human nature.

Nitobe then tells a quick narrative by Shigemori (pronounced 'shee'-'gay'-'moh'-'ree'), *"If I be loyal, my father must be undone; if I obey my father, my duty to my sovereign must go amiss."* Nitobe poses this dichotomy between clashing loyalties and suggests how a Japanese person would or should typically respond within a traditional, feudal context of Bushido. He states that many are *"torn by the conflict between duty and affection."* Nitobe asserts *"in such conflicts Bushido never wavered in its choice of Loyalty."* But, I do not see this dichotomy as a conflict between duty and affection. I see this plainly as conflicting commitments. In such a scenario, I must evaluate the situation and determine which party is right and which party is wrong (or perhaps, which party is most right and which is more wrong). The conflict can be resolved merely by objective evaluation and, if necessary, side with the party I conclude to be right, or most right. If I were to discover, for example, that my son had committed a premeditated murder outside of a self-defense context, I would certainly turn him in to the authorities even though I would still feel strong affection toward him. I would do so not because I should be loyal to the authorities, but because it would simply be the right thing to do. Of course, this is easy for me to say since I do not have children.

According to Nitobe, *"Women, too, encouraged their offspring to sacrifice all for the sovereign ... the Samurai matron stood ready to give up her boys for the cause of Loyalty."* In America, we might call this brainwashing and/or a social disorder. Parents who encourage this kind of behavior are often shunned and socially-ostracized, if not, charged with child endangerment. At the very least, Child Protective Services are contacted.

Nitobe argues that the notion of absolute Loyalty to one's lord or the sovereign (i.e. the Japanese Emperor) is an ethical outcome of the Confucian-based political theory that a nation-state precedes the individual and, therefore, the individual is subordinate to and must be willing to sacrifice one's own life at a moment's notice for the nation-state. However, I think many in Western cultures would challenge this long-held Asian assertion by instead offering for consideration that individuals invented the concept of a nation-state and therefore, in direct contrast to Confucian thought, individuals actually precede the existence of a nation-state. For there can be no nation-state if there are no individuals. A nation-state, in fact, is a product of individuals functioning collectively. One of the primary purposes of creating a nation-state to begin with is to protect the rights of individuals contained within. America, for example, was in many respects founded on this very notion. Therefore, I think the integrity of Nitobe's substantiation for absolute Loyalty to the sovereign or a lord fails when viewed from this perspective.

So, in a modern day martial arts context, must a student demonstrate this kind of extreme and absolute Loyalty to their martial arts teacher(s) in order to live congruently with the philosophy of Bushido? What of circumstances relating to misplaced Loyalty and/or the existence of inappropriate, unethical, even illegal behaviors committed or suggested by one's superiors? Should a student still offer unquestioned, absolute Loyalty to their school or instructors? Let's discuss.

The reason why I propose that Nitobe's articulation of feudal Loyalty is obsolete today has to do with the reason, motivation and purpose behind martial arts training then and martial arts training today. In feudal Japan, people were trained as Samurai for the sole purpose of protecting a lord and/or acting in the service of a sovereign. However, that is *not at all* why anyone from Western cultures or Japan (in all likelihood) engages in martial arts training today. In modern society, people engage in martial arts training overwhelmingly for *selfish* purposes. Many seek *self*-defense skills, but others want *self*-improvement. It could be improvement of one's *personal* fitness, *self*-esteem, *self*-confidence, spirit or even just to have fun while learning a cultural art. And, it should also be acknowledged that these self-oriented benefits are heavily marketed to the public by a large percentage of martial arts schools in Western cultures today. The one thing all of these motivations have in common is the self. They are all selfish motivations of the person seeking martial arts training. In almost no circumstances do people who seek out martial arts training expect to lay down their life in the service of a superior lord or sovereign. I suppose one could argue that one might seek out martial arts training for purposes of becoming involved in law enforcement, the military, or other security-related services; however, people primarily do this for the exchange of financial compensation, and therefore, these individuals are acting more in the capacity of a mercenary than a loyal servant to a superior. Undoubtedly then, this fundamental change in motive will have substantial impacts on both the definition and application of Bushido's Loyalty in modern society.

Loyalty, as it existed in feudal Japan, does not exist anymore; and, in my opinion, nor should it. Human beings of all cultures around the world have outgrown this antiquated and oppressive relationship dynamic. It could possibly be argued that the Japanese feudal system approximated in many respects equivalence to American slavery, which, of course, was an embarrassing and shameful period in American history. Therefore, as a natural and logical consequence of this obsolete system, this feudal incarnation of Loyalty no longer has any place in the precepts of modern day Bushido. But does this mean that the entire virtue of Loyalty is irrelevant? Of course, not.

Over the years and from time to time, I have had business partners, colleagues, employers, and martial arts teachers take advantage of me, abusing the relationship that existed between us. And as such, any sense of duty or Loyalty I may have had to those individuals promptly dissolved. In the past, for example, I had been asked to ostracize a fellow martial arts student just because my martial arts teacher at the time didn't have the Rectitude, Courage or Politeness to confront the student about a rift that existed between the two of them. This behavior was unacceptable to me. I expressed my disappointment with the teacher then voluntarily left the school; and with my departure so, too, did any Loyalty or sense of duty that existed prior to the abusiveness.

Another martial arts teacher I formerly associated with expected me to operate our school in a capacity that would require me to break the law. This, too, was unacceptable and my Loyalty to and association with that teacher subsequently and immediately vanished. If I were to follow the precepts of feudal Bushido, I would have been expected to either engage in the unacceptable behavior or my only other option would be to kill myself. I would have been required to punish myself for someone else's wrong-doing. Both of these options are, of course, unacceptable in the 21st century. This barbaric, nonsensical behavior from an extinct time would be utterly irresponsible to both me and my family in today's socio-economic culture and environment. Furthermore, I couldn't care less if I were thought of as disloyal by those whom I no longer have a responsibility or commitment toward. For a martial arts teacher, employer, or any other superior to expect such actions of unquestioned, absolute Loyalty is, in my opinion, inappropriate and, well, just plain delusional.

So then, of what definition and in what form should Loyalty be understood and exercised today? In similar fashion to other virtues we have explored, I propose exhibiting an intra-personal dynamic or self-Loyalty —

that is, one should have a duty and responsibility to be loyal to oneself and to one's fundamental understanding of and adherence to right and wrong. We, too, should submit to the command of a higher voice. However, the higher voice I refer to is not that of another person, deity, or community, but the higher voice within each of us. It is our highest self that tells us what to do (or not do) on a daily basis. We always know what the right thing to do is because, as Larry Winget in a previous chapter put it, it is almost always the harder of the two things we are deciding between. It is to this highest self that we must be most loyal to.

John Cornvino, an associate professor of philosophy at Wayne State University argues that *"loyalty is only a virtue to the extent that the object of loyalty is good."* In other words, how tolerant should an employee be of an employer's shortcomings? For example, many years ago a good friend of mine was working for a prominent aviation company on the East Coast. After some time, he discovered some illegal behaviors that the company was engaging in and my friend was being asked to be complicit in those behaviors. He was expected to be a "loyal" employee, support the company action and so on. However, this was not acceptable to him. He began documenting the illegal behavior and eventually became a whistle-blower for the industry. What he did was not *loyal to the company*, but was *loyal to himself*. I doubt anyone would consider him a bad or weak person for not being an unquestioning, absolutely loyal employee. In fact, many, including myself, think of him as a courageous hero. I regard my friend as courageous because he demonstrated knowledge, composure, preparation and

Loyalty

right-reasoning in his action; all inherent characteristics of Courage and Rectitude.

With regard to my two martial arts experiences summarized in earlier paragraphs of this chapter, I had an obligation to myself to do what I deemed right and just, not to do whatever some alleged "superior" instructed or encouraged me to do. By the way, adherence to feudal Loyalty wouldn't hold up in court now would it? *"Your Honor, I was just doing what my Sensei asked me to do."* I believe the response from the magistrate would fall along the lines of, *"What are you, a child!?"* This also reminds me of a much-repeated adage from my parents when I was ten years-old, *"If someone told you to jump off the Brooklyn Bridge, would you do that, too?"*

The problem with romanticizing and caricaturizing obsolete and injurious conceptions such as unquestioned, absolute Loyalty and carrying them forth into today's modern society is that it obscures clear thinking and the proper delineation of right and wrong. Furthermore, it inappropriately absolves all responsibility from the junior person in the relationship from having to make any difficult, mature, and adult-oriented decisions. Life is full of circumstances where people must make difficult decisions; and adhering to unquestioned, absolute Loyalty is one way to avoid having to act like an adult, particularly in the presence of inappropriate behaviors. This historical, culturally-reinforced behavior is simply unacceptable in the 21st century in any country. As such, Bushido's interpretation and application of Loyalty must evolve.

In today's Western society, priorities are different than they were back in feudal Japan. I, for example, have a very strong commitment to my martial arts training and I am very loyal to my martial arts teachers. However, I am first loyal to my own personal virtues, i.e. I have my priorities straight. Martial arts training is quaternary in importance in my life. My health comes first; my family comes second; my livelihood comes third; and martial arts training is a distant fourth. If a member of my family became severely ill requiring me to step away from my training that would be an easy and obvious decision for me. Similarly, if any of my teachers' spouses or families had similar predicaments, I would expect no less from them. Does this mean I am not loyal to my teachers? Does this mean they are not loyal to their students? Of course, not. It just means we are all modern-day, Western-culture adults with our priorities straight. I've seen teachers throw students out of martial arts schools when circumstances like these happen in their students' lives and I can think of nothing more inappropriately selfish on the part of those teachers. This is shameful behavior.

Martial arts training is a powerful and beneficial system of education in today's world, but let's recognize that it certainly isn't required for day-to-day survival, at least not in most Western societies. Does this mean that people from those Western cultures and values cannot demonstrate Loyalty or follow the precepts of Bushido? Once again, absolutely, not.

One should remain steadfastly loyal in a committed relationship (e.g. student-teacher, spouse-spouse, employee-employer) so long as both parties in that relationship acutely remember and abide by the nature and expectations of the relationship – as long as neither party takes the relationship for granted or pushes beyond the proper boundaries of the relationship. In other words, in today's world, *Loyalty is conditional;* whereas Loyalty was unconditional in feudal Japan. It was unconditional because people had no choice, save the taking of their own life and, in many cases, they even required permission from their lord to do that! So, in all honesty, they truly had no choice or freedom to be loyal. Freedom of choice is the crucial element distinguishing modern Bushido's Loyalty from feudal Bushido's Loyalty. Personally, I think this is a positive evolution of this virtue.

Many of today's scholars insist that choice without duress is a fundamental characteristic of Loyalty. Richard Mullin, professor of philosophy at Wheeling Jesuit University, asserts that *"loyalty is willing in that it is freely given, not coerced."* This characteristic would conflict with the Japanese socio-economic system that existed during the hey-day of feudal Bushido. It is attributed to Mullin that *"Loyalty is ... chosen after personal consideration, not something that one is born into."* That is worth repeating: *"after personal consideration."* This is another interesting characteristic of Loyalty that Mullin introduces and is conspicuously absent from Nitobe's dissertation. In other, more concise language: forced Loyalty is false Loyalty.

When does this process of personal consideration end? Once you commit to someone? How about after the point of commitment? What if you discover the Loyalty you assigned to someone was inappropriate? Are you too late and stuck with being loyal to this person for perpetuity? What if you subsequently discover after the fact that the person you assigned Loyalty to isn't worthy of your Loyalty? Or, in my friend's work experience described earlier, the senior person engages in inappropriate or illegal behavior? An Internet encyclopedia, addresses the notion of misplaced Loyalty stating that *"Misplaced loyalty is loyalty placed in other persons ... where that loyalty is not acknowledged or respected; is betrayed or taken advantage of."* None of these important attributes of Loyalty are even remotely addressed in Nitobe's articulation of Loyalty. In fact, the more I explore the issue of Loyalty, the more convinced I become that feudal Bushido's virtue of Loyalty was more an artificial construct of Japan's governing powers and their efforts at controlling the thoughts and behaviors of the Samurai class, more so than the outlining of a virtuous, moral code of behavior for an individual.

It is attributed to Stephen Nathanson, professor of philosophy at Northeastern University that *"loyalty can be given to persons that are unworthy. Moreover, loyalty can lead patriots to support policies that are immoral and inhumane... Patriotic loyalty can sometimes rather be a vice than a virtue, when its consequences exceed the boundaries of what is otherwise morally desirable. Such loyalties are erroneously unlimited in their scope and fail to acknowledge boundaries of morality."* A perfect example of this would be Nazi Germany's genocide campaign of World War II. These individuals were steadfastly loyal to their sovereign and their country, but obviously, they were behaving outside the boundaries of morality. Thus it is clear that contemporary Loyalty, unlike the Loyalty of feudal Bushido, is conditional and is only appropriate and acceptable when the actions and intentions of the 'Sempai,' sovereign, teacher, or employer are morally desirable and/or virtuous.

Wim Vandekerckhove, a senior lecturer at the University of Greenwich points out that *"in the late 20th century there sprung forth the notion of bi-directional Loyalty between employees and employers. Previous thinking had encompassed the idea that employees are [to be] loyal to an employer, but not that an employer need be loyal to employees."* This concept did not exist prior to the 20th century, but does and certainly should today. Since feudal systems no longer exist in Western cultures, relationships of senior-to-junior, or 'Sempai-Kohai' (as the Japanese refer to it), should recognize this dynamic and the bi-directional responsibilities contained therein. It is not one to be forgotten, taken for granted, or abused by either party.

For example, another past East Coast friend of mine, who owned a martial arts school, was venting to me one day about how some of his students aren't loyal enough to him. *"Where's the respect?"* he said. Even though he was 20 years my senior, and was a 'Sempai' of mine, I reminded him that Loyalty and Respect are things that are earned, not automatically given just because a person signs up for martial arts classes with a high-ranking black belt. Both students and teachers often forget that there are reciprocal responsibilities of both parties when people enter into an oral contract with one another. The responsibilities do not fall solely on the junior person. My well-intentioned friend had, to an extent, forgotten some of his responsibilities to his students, which was contributing to his perceived predicament.

Martial arts teachers and students who insist upon practicing feudal Bushido in modern times greatly run the risk of exhibiting xenophobic tendencies — the fear of people who are different from one's self and/or, according to Nathanson, the idea that *"all loyalties bar one's own are considered illegitimate."* This is a position not

Inner Bushido

likely to reflect positively on the martial arts community and is the product of excessive efforts at conformism and homogeneity — the insistence that all of your students, peers, and associates be exactly like you. Unfortunately, I have already noticed that those teachers who practice this feudal incarnation of Bushido often find themselves self-quarantined from peers and the community as a whole. If they do this for too long they will find themselves with just a handful of students, if any. Indeed, I have even witnessed martial arts schools collapse over embracement of this antiquated attitude.

I disagree with much of what Nitobe suggests Loyalty represents. However, there was one aspect of Loyalty he describes that I connect with very strongly. Nitobe makes a very strong distinction between being loyal and, for lack of a better word, being a sycophant or kiss-ass to one's lord. He strongly asserts that Bushido despised sucking up. *"Bushido did not require us [Japanese] to make our conscience the slave of any lord or king;"* and *"A man who sacrificed his own conscience to the capricious will or freak or fancy of a sovereign was accorded a low place in the estimate of the Precepts [of Bushido]."*

It took me a while to finally grasp the subtle distinction Nitobe was making, which, once again, is a cultural one. What I think he was getting at was a distinction between a loyal Samurai's *actions* and a Samurai's *thoughts*. Nitobe claims that while Loyalty is owed to one's lord *in action*, Loyalty is not necessarily owed to one's lord *in thought* or spirit. In other words, a lord may be able to force you to do something, but he cannot make you condone that action. This is congruent with a dynamic the Japanese refer to as 'Tatemae' and 'Honne.' This is where a person shows or expresses an abbreviated or superficial side of himself in public ('Tatemae') and expresses in private his true, unfiltered intentions or opinions only to himself or to his close inner circle of friends, family, and colleagues ('Honne'). In Japanese culture this is considered normal, acceptable, even polite behavior. However, although we too often engage in this kind of behavior in the United States, we often call this two-faced, disingenuous, cowardly, or I say with tongue-in-cheek, just "being a politician."

So, is Loyalty antiquated? That depends. Unquestioned Loyalty to others is certainly antiquated. However, to accurately exhibit this virtue in contemporary society we must remember that:

1. **Loyalty is owed first to oneself (the intra-personal dynamic); it is an acute and intra-personal awareness of one's highest self and acting in accordance with one's understanding of right and wrong;**
2. **Loyalty to another person (the inter-personal dynamic) is a conditional relationship based on the adherence to the non-coercive, inherent bidirectional responsibilities and expectations of that relationship; and**
3. **Loyalty should never cross the line to sycophantry.**

時代

CHAPTER NINE: TRANSITION & EVOLUTION

Were the evolution of Bushido to be represented on a timeline between the 11th century and present day, the publishing of Nitobe's 1899 book, in my opinion, would be the symbolic event in history signifying the end of feudal Bushido and the beginning of modern Bushido. As might be expected, this date closely coincides with the official decommissioning of the Samurai class in 1868, the beginning of what is known as the Meiji Restoration. Were it not for the events beginning in 1868, it is possible that Nitobe may not have felt comfortable or safe enough to challenge and criticize the Samurai the way he did. His book might not have ever come to fruition and a tremendous resource for humanity would be lost to us.

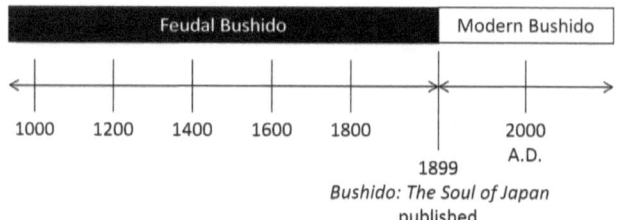

Just as a person's eyes can appear to change color depending upon what color outfit they may be wearing, Bushido, too, takes on a different appearance depending upon its environment. Bushido within a context of 18th century Eastern feudalism looks one way; Bushido within a context of 21st century Western capitalism and democracy looks another way. Furthermore, attempting to practice Bushido in an 18th century Eastern feudalistic context, while living in a capitalistic society of the 21st century, is not only impossible, but inappropriate. More than just inappropriate, it can be downright destructive. Imagine teaching Western youth today that the appropriate, mature, and Bushido-like response to failing at something or committing a shameful act (as all children do) is to cut open one's belly and have a good friend behead you. This may have been socially-acceptable for adults during Japan's 11th-19th centuries (although I might still disagree with this assertion), but by no means would it be considered appropriate today. In fact, assisted suicide is illegal in the United States and other countries, at least at the time of this writing. The point is that any system of thought, values, or morality must be considered in context to its environment.

When I started out writing this series of essays, I had been somewhat jaded by a number of personal experiences over the past 20 years that substantially shook my confidence that Bushido was a legitimate system of values worth studying and following. I was losing confidence in the philosophy because of the repeated behaviors I observed by some in martial arts communities. To try to address the issue, I took up reading numerous books on the subject, including the original text of Inazo Nitobe's *Bushido: The Soul of Japan* because I thought I had a bone to pick with Bushido, and I really did intend on writing a heavily critical review. However, what I discovered in my journey was that, overwhelmingly, it was not Nitobe's text that I disagreed with so much as it was the stereotypical misperceptions and misinterpretations of Bushido imparted today by sometimes well-intentioned, but under-educated martial arts students and teachers. I was pleasantly surprised to conclude that Bushido is, in fact, alive and well today even in the absence of its born environment: feudalism.

It has become clear to me that the overwhelming majority of Bushido enthusiasts (I would hazard a guess of greater than 95%) have never bothered to study Bushido intellectually and have explored the tenets of Bushido only superficially, if at all. They tend to think that as long as they train a martial art and have watched a handful of Samurai movies, starring actors such as Toshiro Mifune or even Hiroyuki Sanada, or have visited Japan, that they understand and are a good representative of Bushido philosophy. This narrow curriculum and presumption seems to be even more abused and pronounced if that martial arts student happens to have a teacher of Asian ethnicity. However, to assume that a teacher has a firm understanding of Bushido just because of their ethnicity is inappropriate and, if we're being honest, even borders on racial prejudice, albeit a positively-intended prejudice. I certainly don't assume that one has to be of Italian heritage to cook the best pasta dishes! Furthermore, just because someone of any ethnicity teaches martial arts today and/or is a high-ranking black belt in their art is not necessarily a good measure or indication of their appreciation for or comprehension and practice of Bushido. This erroneous deduction would largely account for the distorted understanding and promotion of Bushido today across many martial arts schools in many countries.

Many people attracted to the allure of the Samurai (and the Samurai are indeed alluring) appear to have made the Samurai out to be much more than they actually were; and that the seven virtues many attribute to the Samurai were not necessarily well-developed, understood, or actually practiced by the majority of Samurai during their reign. In fact, their origin described by Nitobe as crude braggarts lacking any refinement has been successfully and, by and large, posthumously rehabilitated by authors of more recent decades, to that of guru-like, near-mythological giants. Nitobe's 1899 treatise, on the other hand, poignantly educates readers that the actual practice of the Samurai class was in all likelihood far from the professed philosophic ideals that are commonly attributed to the class today. Just as religious stories and cultural folklore grow, expand, change and exaggerate over time, so too has the legend of the Samurai.

As a result of this sanitization, contemporary peoples (particularly martial arts enthusiasts) have somewhat subconsciously assigned to the Samurai the historical responsibility of preserving and exemplifying virtues

Transition & Evolution

of contemporary martial arts that may not have existed across the Samurai class or populace at the time of their existence. However, that does not lessen in any way the value of those virtues as we strive to practice and achieve them today. There certainly is value in theoretic ideals and just because perfection is not actually attainable does not mean that we shouldn't strive for it.

Nonetheless, many martial artists will continue to profess that they follow and adhere to the "ancient" tenets of Japanese Bushido, so let's address this notion plainly, once and for all. If you lived in feudal Japan 400 years ago and your lord told you to commit suicide, you were required to oblige; that is, if you wanted to retain your and your family's so-called "Honor." This purportedly "courageous" act was a major element and practice of feudal Bushido. You would be required to carry out your lord's commands no matter how outrageous because you were not free to object. Coercion was a major element of the Japanese feudal system. As a whole, people were not free to choose their destinies.

Now, let's fast forward to the present day. If your martial arts teacher, landlord, parent, employer, or governing official (i.e. your analogous lord) told you to commit suicide or to go kill another person, my question to you is: Would you do it? Of course, not. You'd tell him or her to go take a hike. At least, I hope you would. That is because our capitalistic, democratic society permits us the right to choose the direction of our lives without interference or consequence from others. I know this scenario sounds silly and extreme. That's because it is. Today, behaving in this feudal-like capacity would be inappropriate. In fact, it was equally inappropriate back then, but that is for some reason forgotten or ignored by many today. Therefore, this practice, this characteristic, this element of Bushido is equally silly and inappropriate. So why don't we martial artists collectively and simultaneously agree to abandon the inane assertion that one practices "old school" Bushido. No one does. If they do, they go to jail.

Instead, we all in martial arts today practice *modern* Bushido, which among many other notions discussed throughout this book includes not forfeiting your intelligence and ability to think or subordinating your personal autonomy to another. Today's Bushido is about serving one's self. That is, it is about your commitment to yourself, the development of yourself, the preservation of yourself and the enjoyment for yourself. You may possess and demonstrate substantial commitment, Honor, Respect, humility, and deference to your school, teachers and fellow students. However, never do you subordinate your personal autonomy. Ultimately, you are there by choice and for your benefit.

The notion of engaging in antiquated practices associated with feudal Bushido only seems romantic when we suspend our disbelief and fantasize as children do of an extinct world where the consequences of our actions are irrelevant and removed from present day reality. When we actually contemplate behaving that way in the 21st century, these same fantasized behaviors seem morbidly inappropriate and even embarrassing. Feudalism has overwhelmingly failed as a system of governance for many reasons. It was both morally wrong and culturally unsustainable, to name just two. So let's all try to keep some perspective when thumping our chests in front of others purporting to following "old school" feudal Bushido or condemning fellow martial artists for differences in our chosen, modern expressions of our respective arts.

Just as the outward manifestations and practices of Bushido in 1514 were probably very different than the manifestations and practices of Bushido in 1814, so too, shall the outward manifestations and practices of Bushido be in 2014 (the year of this publication). We must not forget that in order to survive all things must change, grow, and evolve. Bushido is no exception. It is neither necessarily good, nor possible to practice Bushido today as it was in feudal Japan. Nonetheless, we can still preserve and continue to grow and evolve the spirit of Bushido, but we must be mature enough to abandon illogical, adverse, or otherwise poor manifestations, behaviors, and comprehensions of Bushido's virtues. Instead, we must utilize Bushido's philosophy to grow as human beings, not use so-called Bushido to hide behind as a shield for failing to address personal insecurities.

Bushido (or martial arts in general) is a wonderful system of education that benefits millions of people around the world and should be perpetuated in a modern context. We must remember that modern Bushido is an intra-personal journey. It is not a system of thought that should be used to pass judgment upon others. It is one thing to misunderstand one or more virtues of Bushido within a context of self-analysis. This can be easily remedied with some careful, attentive study and practice. However, it is entirely another thing to attempt to judge, to censure, and to hold other people accountable for *your* misunderstanding and misuse of those virtues.

Inner Bushido

It is our — the martial arts community's — responsibility to make sure that the tenets of Bushido continue to grow and evolve with our perpetually-evolving humanity and not stagnate in dogma or serve as a tool for indulging other peoples' perceived inadequacies. There is nothing "traditional" or "authentic" about endorsing and promulgating antiquated, inane behaviors that violate basic principles of ethics and an innate sense of right and wrong.

Nitobe's book on the virtues of Bushido was a powerful literary expression for the end of the 19th century. However, I speculate that many readers in the 21st century would struggle with his, by today's standards, somewhat arcane writing style reminiscent of esoteric academics of the Victorian era. Nitobe's original work can be difficult to relate to as it is filled with an immensely impressive vocabulary not commonly used today, as well as an extensive use of social and other pop-culture references relevant and unique to his day. These bear little communicative value in the 21st century. The book you hold in your hands is an effort to update his concepts, essentially "translating" his dissertation from 19th century English to 21st century English to help preserve his poignant concepts and observations.

Even though Westerners, particularly Americans, tend to favor short, concise summaries as opposed to lengthy explorations of thought, this small book ended up being rather verbose itself despite my best efforts. To appeal to that constituency, the following summary and illustrations are my further attempts to consolidate, yet still fairly and accurately represents the tenets of modern Bushido as I believe Nitobe articulated in 1899. Please note, however, that no philosophy of any value can be boiled down to what I called "bumper-sticker" axioms without losing some degree of acumen.

Modern Bushido: At-a-Glance Summary

Rectitude   means living with integrity, within right reasoning and free from guilt

Courage   means doing the hard thing and demonstrating Moral Courage

Benevolence   means feeling the distress of others and exercising restraint in judgment of others

Politeness   means accumulating power through the graceful, economical expression of manners

Truthfulness   means adhering to one's perfect word and recognizing the existence of multiple truths

Honor   means possessing self-respect and segregating that self-respect from ego

Loyalty   means listening to one's highest self and not behaving as a sycophant

In conclusion to this dissertation, I offer the following:

While I benefited greatly from Nitobe's metaphor of a symmetrical arch (presented earlier) to illustrate the anatomy of Bushido's virtues, I felt that the metaphor lacked an accurate visual articulation of the relationship each virtue bears to one another. Therefore, I propose another illustration, one that I hope will more accurately represent the interconnectedness of Bushido's virtues as well as illuminate the unique attributes that influence, or are affected by, each virtue.

The most recognizable symbol of Japanese Bushido is, without doubt, the 'Katana,' the curved, long sword of the Samurai. However, rather than utilize the most obvious element of the 'Katana,' the blade, I suggest that we converge our focus upon the hand guard or 'Tsuba' portion of the 'Katana' to visually summarize Bushido's virtues. The 'Tsuba' is a protective device of the 'Katana.' The function of the 'Tsuba' is two-fold: first, it protects from an opponent's weapon sliding down the blade of the swordsman and injuring his or her hands; and second, the 'Tsuba' acts as a barrier protecting the swordsman from inadvertently grasping the sharp, blade portion of his or her own sword. I elected to use the 'Tsuba' as a symbol for illustrating Bushido's virtues because Bushido's virtues act in a similar fashion, as a safeguard from error, misuse and abuse. Like a 'Katana,' Bushido can be dangerous if used inappropriately or carelessly. The adjacent illustration is not comprehensive by any means, but does effectively summarize the crux of the relationships between the virtues.

Transition & Evolution

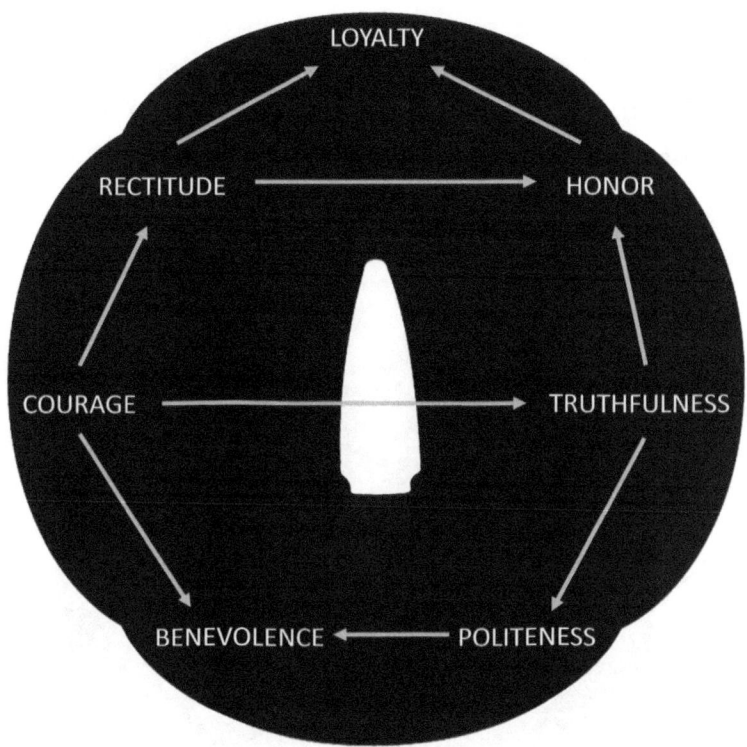

In no particular order, this illustration can be read as:

- Courage is a prerequisite of Rectitude, Truthfulness and Benevolence
- Rectitude is a prerequisite of both Honor and Loyalty
- Truthfulness is a prerequisite of Honor and Politeness
- Honor must precede Loyalty
- Benevolence is the outward expression of Politeness

Inner Bushido

Furthermore, these virtues each originate from, or are at least influenced by, other attributes that facilitate the philosophy of Bushido, but are not considered by Nitobe to be virtues in and of themselves. These important attributes can be added to our Bushido 'Tsuba' illustration.

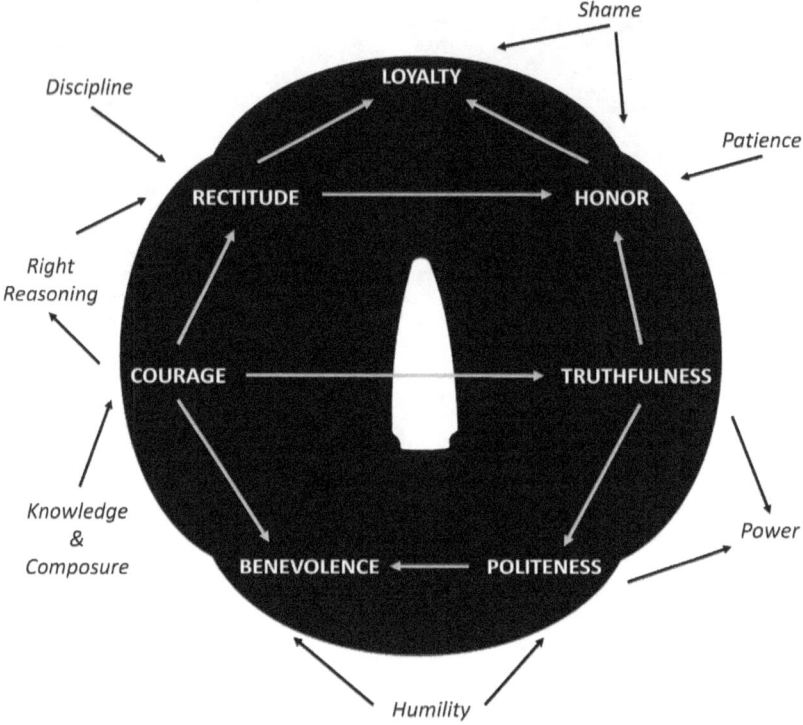

Again, in no particular order, this illustration can be read as:

- Discipline and right reasoning represent the path to cultivating Rectitude
- Courage is the virtue responsible for preserving Right Reasoning or 'Giri'

- Knowledge and Composure are critical prerequisites for forging Courage
- Humility is an influencing element of both Benevolence and Politeness
- Power is a combined product of the virtues of Truthfulness and Politeness
- Patience is an inherent quality of Honor
- Shame is a driving force behind Loyalty and Honor

I wish you the best of luck in your martial training, personal development and continued study of Bushido's virtues and attributes.

'Masagatsu agatsu'
"True victory, is victory over oneself!"
— Morihei Ueshiba, The Founder of Aikido

BONUS CHAPTER: TRUTHFULNESS (CONTINUED)

BUSHIDO & COMMERCE

Let's begin this bonus chapter by expanding upon the material covered in the chapter on Truthfulness and become familiar with some of Nitobe's opinions and positions on Bushido and what its relationship was to Japanese commerce of the late 19th century. Occasionally, I shall interject and offer support or a rebuttal.

"It may not be wrong to devote a few words to commercial integrity ... A loose business morality has indeed been the worst blot on our [Japanese] national reputation ... Of all the great occupations of life, none was farther removed from the profession of arms than commerce. The merchant was placed

119

lowest in the category of vocations (In order: The knight, the farmer, the mechanic or artisan, and the merchant)."

"The Samurai derived his income from land and could even indulge in amateur farming, but the counter and abacus were abhorred ... We knew the wisdom of this social arrangement." According to Nitobe, Charles Montesquieu, a French political thinker of The Enlightenment, well-known for his articulation of the theory of the separation of powers *"advocated the prevention of nobility from mercantile pursuits, believing that it would prevent wealth from accumulating in the hands of the powerful ... The separation of power and riches kept the distribution of riches more nearly equable."* I'm unconvinced that history has ever proved this dynamic to be effective or wise. I'm quite certain, however, that historically and presently, those who have riches are the ones in power. Certainly, Morihei Ueshiba, the Founder of Aikido, was a powerful person physically, socially, and in the respect he commanded by his peers and disciples, but that isn't really the socio-economic power Nitobe is discussing here.

It has been suggested that *"one cause of the decadence of the Roman Empire, was the permission given to the nobility to engage in trade."* What I don't understand is: Who exactly would grant permission to nobility to engage in a pursuit other than nobility themselves? If the merchant class were the only ones to have the right to accumulate riches, wouldn't the merchants simply become the class of power? In fact, isn't that exactly what happened to Japan? The Samurai lost their power because they failed, in part, to remain relevant to society, one of those relevancies being that they failed to participate in the new economy and culture. The

Bushido & Commerce

Samurai lost their "wealth" and "currency," so to speak, associated with knighthood. They lost their status in society as protectors because they were no longer valued by society. Almost overnight, upon Japanese ports being opened to trade with foreign countries, the Samurai lost their "cultural currency" as the populace switched what they valued from physical protection and sustenance to the equitable exchange of goods and services. The truth of the matter is that the Samurai are extinct largely because of their failure to adapt to the proletariat-like movement happening around them. They failed as a class, in part, because of their conceit and an over-developed sense of entitlement in the face of a rapidly-changing environment.

I object to the Samurai attitude towards tradesman presented by Nitobe. I think being a tradesman requires a code of morals equal to, but not necessarily greater than or less than, that of any other class including Samurai. Let's not forget that for all of their high and lofty beliefs about themselves, Samurai are extinct and the merchant class is not, which means the Samurai ultimately failed to succeed in life. Perhaps then we should think twice before trying to emulate their behavior unless we, too, desire to extinguish ourselves.

"It is unnecessary to add that no business, commercial or otherwise, can be transacted without a code of morals. Our merchants of the feudal period had one among themselves, without which they never could have developed, as they did, such fundamental mercantile institutions [such] as the guild, the bank ... insurance, checks, bills of exchange, etc.; but in their relations with people outside their vocation, the tradesmen lived too true to the reputation of their order [profession]." This

makes no sense and, in my opinion, it is just sour grapes. There is no reason to treat people in commerce differently from one another – those who do quickly find themselves with commerce difficulties.

Is Nitobe really trying to blame the merchant class for the Samurai's failure to assimilate to the new cultural currency? If the newly-engaged-in-commerce Samurai class were not welcomed or trusted by the merchant class, this may have been due, in part, to the decades, even centuries-long poor treatment and lack of respect for the merchant class by the Samurai. After all, according to Nitobe the Samurai considered merchants to be the lowest, least-respected class of Japanese society. I don't know, this sounds a bit like appropriate, proportional karma to me. We all reap what we sow. Or to put it in a maxim more relatable to the Samurai, *"Live by the sword; die by the sword."*

"Only a few years after our treaty ports were opened to foreign trade, feudalism was abolished, and when with it the Samurai's fiefs were taken and bonds issued to them in compensation, they were given liberty to invest them in mercantile transactions. Now you may ask, 'Why could they not bring their much boasted veracity [Truthfulness] into their new business relations and so reform the old abuses?'" poses Nitobe. *"... many a noble and honest Samurai who signally and irrevocably failed in his new and unfamiliar field of trade and industry, through sheer lack of shrewdness in coping with his artful plebeian rival. When we know that 80% of the business houses fail in so industrial a country as America, is it any wonder that scarcely one in one-hundred Samurai who went into trade could succeed in his new vocation?"* To this I must say, so what! This approximates the same

Bushido & Commerce

percentage of success any other merchant or business person in any other country has when entering commerce. In fact, an 80% failure rate is quite generous. In America today, more than 95% of businesses fail within 5 years. Is Nitobe really suggesting that the Samurai class receive favored treatment or subsidization? Nitobe is simply grousing on behalf of the extinct culture, advocating a spoiled sense of entitlement among a former ruling class that had (perhaps appropriately) lost power to a more adaptive, evolving class of society.

Nitobe unconvincingly attempts to create the argument that Samurai failed to adapt to the abolishment of feudalism and the shifting of class power because of their holier than thou virtues, their sense of Truthfulness being greater or better than that of another class. However, in my opinion, it was actually this very belief — that they were superior to other classes of people and that the rules of survival and labors of society shouldn't apply to them — that contributed heavily to their cultural demise. In this portion of his Truthfulness essay, Nitobe repeatedly makes the insinuation that Samurai were honest and tradesman and merchants were dishonest. As a tradesman I find this position perplexingly sad. I don't take offense to it because it simply isn't true. In this article, Nitobe creates, perhaps unintentionally, the impression that all Samurai were honest. Such certainly was not the case. Samurai, like any other kind of people, are just human. All of whom are susceptible to the vast array of weaknesses that define us as human beings.

"It will be long before it will be recognized how many fortunes were wrecked in the attempt to apply Bushido ethics to business methods," says Nitobe. This statement is a

diversion, a red herring, if you will. I consistently apply Bushido ethics to business methods and find that the two work very well together and are, in fact, necessary to succeed in business in many respects. Nitobe continues, *"...but it was soon patent to every observing mind that the ways of wealth were not ways of Honor."* Here Nitobe is simply wrong, making a broad-brushed, prejudiced statement offending an entire class of tradesman, deliberately intended to distract attention away from the likely fact that the privileged Samurai class overwhelmingly failed to succeed in a new socio-economic climate.

Certainly, it is possible that Nitobe's assessment of 19th century Japanese commerce ethic is a fair and accurate representation. Perhaps, as a whole, the ethics and business morality of the merchant class were shady. I do not know, of course. I wasn't there. In fact, none of us were. However, the reason why I so strongly object to Nitobe's mantra that *"the ways of wealth were not the ways of Honor"* is because of its potential ramification in the 21st century. If a person today were to read, believe, and advocate in the 21st century Nitobe's 19th century opinions on Bushido and commerce, I'm afraid it would lend a black eye to those of us who practice Bushido. For a person today to endorse the notion that the ways of wealth are not the ways of Honor would be grossly inappropriate. This fallacy cannot be left to stand or go unchallenged and be carried forth to present day.

Are we really supposed to feel sympathy for the strong, bellicosely-trained Samurai class, who managed to belligerently hold on to power as a ruling class in Japan for 900 years, just because they failed in business as often as anyone else from the merchant class did? Were

Bushido & Commerce

the poor, military-trained warriors of yesteryear really defeated by the measly merchants? Are we seriously supposed to feel sorry for the Samurai in this scenario? That they failed to succeed in business because they were chronically honest? Does this *really* make sense?

Today, in the United States, the military is constantly promoting the importance and value of military service and training in the business world. In fact, one of the most impressive assets an employer can see on a résumé is military service. In today's world, military service complements the business world. It doesn't contrast it! But Nitobe would have us believe that the two have nothing to do with one another. If Nitobe's assertive position is representative of the collective disposition of the Samurai class, then Nitobe's massive error in judgment reflects a contributing factor to why the Samurai failed to assimilate to their rapidly-changing world.

As I continue through this chapter of *Bushido: The Soul of Japan*, Nitobe's personal disdain for commerce, which I have often found common among academics, is becoming increasingly evident and I am, respectively, increasingly disappointed with the attempt to adversely juxtapose Bushido with commerce. I feel comfortable making such a criticism about academia since I too am a product of the academic world.

In my opinion, this is where the superficial comprehension of Bushido's values falls flat. Mind you, I don't think Truthfulness is an antiquated Bushido virtue. In fact, quite the contrary. 'Makoto' is so important to me that I have deliberately selected the Japanese character for Truthfulness to be included in our Aikido school's 'Kamon' (crest). However, I do think that the position Nitobe articulates regarding Truthfulness as it relates to commerce and business ethics is neither mature nor sophisticated. Once again, though, it must be remembered that the position he articulates may not be solely his own personal opinion. After all, Nitobe was not Samurai, but an academic, and he may be trying to echo a sentiment that he learned from his Samurai uncle, Ota Tokitoshi, and to whom the book is dedicated.

"With all of my sincere regard for the high commercial integrity of the Anglo-Saxon race," Nitobe says, *"when I ask for the ultimate ground [bottom line], I am told that 'Honesty is the best policy,' that it 'pays to be honest.' Is this virtue, then, not its own reward?"* Yes. Honesty is its own reward, but I would offer that financial equity can be a positive outcome of abundance — that is, a physical symbol of chronic Honesty. Of course, there are also plenty of examples, especially in recent years, of Western companies accruing large amounts of equity through dishonest actions; but to pass judgment on all of commerce for the actions of a few (or admittedly, even more than a few) would be an unfair position to espouse. Money is not the root of all evil. Some would convincingly argue a lack of money is a root of evil. Money can be accrued both honestly and dishonestly.

"If it [this virtue of honesty] is followed because it brings in more cash than falsehood [dishonesty], I am afraid Bushido would rather indulge in lies." This is a humorous, but ultimately idiotic statement by Nitobe. There is no suggestion at all that honesty is followed because it brings in more cash than dishonesty. Honesty is followed by many simply because it is the virtuous thing to do;

and if being honest happens to bring in more cash, then that is just a positive ramification of virtuous behavior. Consider, do people save money *because* it generates more money (through compound interest)? Or do people save money because it is smart and responsible? Compound interest is just a positive effect of saving. One cannot help but detect in Nitobe a prejudicial disposition — what is commonly known today as a "poverty consciousness" or an "addiction to poverty." It is the erroneous belief that poverty is somehow more virtuous than wealth. This is another chronic, psychological condition consistently plaguing some martial arts communities.

"If Bushido rejects a doctrine of quid pro quo rewards [equal exchange of goods and services], the shrewder tradesman will readily accept it." This is intended by Nitobe to be an offensive statement to the merchant class, but what kind of fool would reject a doctrine of quid pro quo? What is the alternative to an equal exchange of value? An *unequal* exchange of value? Nitobe's argument seems to have entirely lost its footing on terra firma and I am inclined to think that perhaps he was a bit heavy into the 'Sake' bottle the night he wrote these passages.

In my opinion, Nitobe's position on Bushido and its relationship to commerce and business ethics is way off-base and any expression of modern Bushido must entirely remove from its canon any reference by Nitobe on this peculiar and tangential position.

ABOUT THE AUTHOR

Sean Hannon began his study of martial arts in the 1980s. He first earned his black belt in Okinawa Karate, began training Japanese Aikido in the 1990s in New Jersey, then continued his Aikido training with schools in Illinois, South Carolina, and Colorado. Sean has had the privilege of training in seminar with many high-ranking instructors from the United States, Japan and other countries.

After a debilitating spinal injury in the mid-2000s that left him unable to walk for over a full year, Sean re-evaluated his priorities and decided that one of the things that made him most happy in life was practicing the art of Aikido. Since there was no Aikido program in his town of residence, he took it upon himself to create an Aikido school or 'Dojo' in Castle Rock, Colorado while he slowly rehabilitated his injury. Today, the school offers programs in multiple traditional, Japanese martial arts.

Sean trains Iaido (pronounced 'ee'-'eye'-'doh'), the art of traditional Japanese sword-drawing, under Iwakabe, Monica Sensei and Iwakabe, Hideki Sensei. In 2013, Sean placed 1st for the Murakami Cup at the annual AUSKF national Iaido competition. He also practices Kyudo, "the Way of the Bow" or Japanese archery, under Shibata, Kanjuro Sensei and his senior students in Boulder, Colorado. Shibata Sensei is a twentieth generation master bow maker, and he was a third generation official bow maker to the Emperor of Japan and the Japanese Imperial Court until his retirement.

A long-term appreciation for the Japanese martial arts has since expanded into a broader appreciation for other elements of Japanese culture. Presently, Sean is learning to speak Japanese and has developed a strong appreciation for 17th - 18th century Japanese woodblock prints called 'Ukiyo-e' (pronounced 'oo'-'kee'-'yo'-'eh') Sean is an avid writer on the subjects of Aikido and classic Japanese martial arts philosophy; and how to apply such in contemporary society. His writings and philosophy have been published and cited in regional, national, and European newspapers, magazines, and professional trade journals.

Visitors are always welcome. If you find yourself visiting the Denver, Colorado area you are welcome to stop by and train with us. Please contact us before you visit.

Castle Rock AIKIDO
Castle Rock, Colorado, USA
(720) 221-3665
www.CRaikido.com

www.ingramcontent.com/pod-product-compliance
Lightning Source LLC
Chambersburg PA
CBHW032041290426
44110CB00012B/902